Cheap AND *Easy!*

WASHING MACHINE REPAIR

2000 EDITION

Written ESPECIALLY for Trade Schools, Do-It-Yourselfers, and other "green" technicians!

By Douglas Emley

EB Publishing, Inc.

Carson City, Nevada ● Phone / Fax toll free 888-974-1224 ● website: http://www.appliancerepair.net

D1119586

S

The Author, the publisher and all interested parties have used all possible care to assure that the information contained in this book is as complete and as accurate as possible. However, neither the publisher nor the author nor any interested party assumes any liability for omissions, errors, or defects in the materials, instructions or diagrams contained in this publication, and therefore are not liable for any damages including (but not limited to) personal injury, property damage or legal disputes that may result from the use of this book.

All major appliances are complex electro-mechanical devices. Personal injury or property damage may occur before, during, or after any attempt to repair an appliance. This publication is intended for individuals posessing an adequate background of technical experience. The above named parties are not responsible for an individual's judgement of his or her own technical abilities and experience, and therefore are not liable for any damages including (but not limited to) personal injury, property damage or legal disputes that may result from such judgements.

The advice and opinions offered by this publication are of a subjective nature ONLY and they are NOT to be construed as legal advice. The above named parties are not responsible for the interpretation or implementation of subjective advice and opinions, and therefore are not responsible for any damages including (but not limited to) personal injury, property damage, or legal disputes that may result from such interpretation or implementation.

The use of this publication acknowledges the understanding and acceptance of the above terms and conditions.

Special Thanks to technical consultants Dick Miller and Jose Hernandez, whose collective decades of experience as field appliance service technicians are reflected in the technical information and procedures described in this publication.

Published by EB Publishing, Inc., 251 Jeanell Drive Suite 3, Carson City, NV 89703

Printed in the United States of America

HOW TO USE THIS BOOK

STEP 1: READ THE DISCLAIMERS ON THE PREVIOUS PAGE. This book is intended for use by people who have a bit of mechanical experience or aptitude, and just need a little coaching when it comes to appliances. If you don't fit that category, don't use this book! We're all bloomin' lawyers these days, y'know? If you break something or hurt yourself, no one is responsible but **YOU**; not the author, the publisher, the guy or the store who sold you this book, or anyone else. Only **YOU** are responsible, and just by using this book, you're agreeing to that. If you don't understand the disclaimers, get a lawyer to translate them **before** you start working.

Read the safety and repair precautions in section 1-5. These should help you avoid making too many *really* bad mistakes.

STEP 2: READ CHAPTERS 1 & 2: Everything else in this book flows from chapters 1 and 2. If you don't read them, you won't be able to properly diagnose your washer.

Know what kind of washer you have and basically how it works. When you go to the appliance parts dealer, have the nameplate information at hand. Have the proper tools at hand, and know how to use them.

STEP 3: READ THE CHAPTER ABOUT YOUR SPECIFIC BRAND AND MODEL.

STEP 4: FIX THE BLOOMIN' THING! If you can, of course. If you're just too confused, or if the book recommends calling a technician for a complex operation, call one.

WHAT THIS BOOK WILL DO FOR YOU
(and what it won't!)

This book **will** tell you how to fix the most common problems with the most common brands of domestic (household) top-loading washing machines. (This represents 95+ percent of all repairs that the average handyman or service tech will run into.)

This book **will not** tell you how to fix your industrial or commercial or any very large washing machine. The support and control systems for such units are usually very similar in function to those of smaller units, but vastly different in design, service and repair.

We **will** show you the easiest and/or fastest method of diagnosing and repairing your washer.

We **will not necessarily** show you the cheapest way of doing something. Sometimes, when the cost of a part is just a few dollars, we advocate replacing the part rather than rebuilding it. We also sometimes advocate replacement of an inexpensive part, whether it's good or bad, as a simplified method of diagnosis or as a preventive measure.

We **will** use only the simplest of tools; tools that a well-equipped home mechanic is likely to have and to know how to use, including a VOM.

We **will not** advocate your buying several hundred dollars' worth of exotic equipment or special tools, or getting advanced technical training to make a one-time repair. It will usually cost you less to have a professional perform this type of repair. Such repairs represent only a very small percentage of all needed repairs.

We **do not** discuss electrical or mechanical theories. There are already many very well-written textbooks on these subjects and most of them are not likely to be pertinent to the job at hand; fixing your washer!

We **do** discuss rudimentary mechanical systems and simple electrical circuits.

We expect you to be able to look at a part and remove it if the mounting bolts and/or connections are obvious. If the mounting mechanism is complicated or hidden, or there are tricks to removing or installing something, we'll tell you about it.

You are expected to know what certain electrical and mechanical devices are, what they do in general, and how they work. For example, switches, relays, motors, solenoids, cams, clutches, brakes, pullies, idlers, belts, helical shafts, radial and thrust (axial) bearings, flexible motor couplings, splines, water valves, water and oil seals, centrifugal pumps, and pressure diaphragms. If you do not know what these things do, learn them BEFORE you start working on your washer.

You should know how to cut, strip, and splice wire with crimp-on connectors, wire nuts and electrical tape. You should know how to measure voltage and how to test for continuity with a VOM (Volt-Ohm Meter). If you have an ammeter, you should know how and where to measure the current in amps. If you don't know how to use these meters, there's a brief course on how to use them (for *our* purposes *only*) in Chapter 1. See section 1-4 before you buy either or both of these meters.

A given procedure was only included in this book if it passed the following criteria:
1) The job is something that the average couch potato can complete in one afternoon, with no prior knowledge of the machine, with tools a normal home handyman is likely to have.
2) The parts and/or special tools required to complete the job are easily found and not too expensive.
3) The problem is a common one; occuring more frequently than just one out of a hundred machines.

Costly repairs which are included in this book if they pass the following criteria:
1) The cost of the repair is still far less than replacing the machine or calling a professional service technician, and
2) The repair is likely to yield a machine that will operate satisfactorily for several more years, or at least long enough to justify the cost.

In certain parts of the book, the author expresses an opinion as to whether the current value of a particular machine warrants making the repair or "scrapping" the machine. Such opinions are to be construed as opinions ONLY and they are NOT to be construed as legal advice. The decision as to whether to take a particular machine out of service depends on a number of factors that the author cannot possibly know and has no control over; therefore, the responsibility for such a decision rests solely with the person making the decision.

I'm sure that a physicist reading this book could have a lot of fun tearing it apart because of my deliberate avoidance and misuse of technical terms. However, this manual is written to simplify the material and inform the novice, not to appease the scientist.

*NOTE: The diagnosis and repair procedures in this manual do not necessarily apply to brand-new units, newly-installed units or recently relocated units. Although they **may** posess the problems described in this manual, washers that have recently been installed or moved are subject to special considerations not taken into account in this manual for the sake of simplicity. Such special considerations include installation parameters, installation location, the possibility of manufacturing or construction defects, damage in transit, and others.*

This manual was designed to assist the novice technician in the repair of home (domestic) washers that have been operating successfully for an extended period of months or years and have only recently stopped operating properly, with no major change in installation parameters or location.

Table Of Contents

CHAPTER 4: WHIRLPOOL DIRECT DRIVE MODELS

CHAPTER 5: OLD-STYLE GENERAL ELECTRIC

CHAPTER 6: GENERAL ELECTRIC FRONT-ACCESS MACHINES

CHAPTER 7: MAYTAG

CHAPTER 8: OLD-STYLE SPEED QUEEN (PRE-1980)

CHAPTER 8a: NEW-STYLE SPEED QUEEN (POST-1980)

CHAPTER 9: NORGE DESIGNS

CHAPTER 10: WCI (WHITE CONSOLIDATED INDUSTRIES)

Chapter 1

WASHER IDENTIFICATION TOOLS AND SAFETY TIPS AND TRICKS

1-1. BRAND IDENTIFICATION

Appliance companies, like most other major industries, have their share of takeovers, buyouts and cross-brand agreements.

Besides the seven primary washer models listed in this book, the following models are covered. In some cases, these models were manufactured by the same companies under a different brand name. In other cases, the companies merged, or one bought the other.

ADMIRAL: Norge

AMANA: Speed Queen

CROSLEY: Norge

FRANKLIN: WCI

FRIGIDAIRE: Uni-Matic, Pulse-Matic and roller drive machines are very old designs, and have not been manufactured recently. They are difficult and expensive to get parts for, and thus are not covered in this book. Since the late 70's, Frigidaire has been manufactured by WCI. WCI fairly recently changed their name back to the Frigidaire Home Products Company, but for the most part they keep marketing products under the same wide array of brand names.

GENERAL ELECTRIC: In 1995, GE started making a new "front access" machine. Unlike the old model, there is no rear access panel on these machines; all the machine internals are accessed through the front. Both are covered in this manual, in chapters 5 and 6.

GIBSON: WCI

HOTPOINT: General Electric

INGLIS: Whirlpool

J.C. PENNEY: General Electric

KELVINATOR: WCI

KENMORE: Whirlpool

KITCHENAID: Whirlpool (direct drive)

MAGIC CHEF: Norge

MAYTAG: Most are covered in Chapter 7. "Performa" models are Norge designed; see Chapter 9.

MONTGOMERY WARD: Norge or WCI.

PENNCREST: General Electric

RCA: General Electric

ROPER: Whirlpool (direct drive)

SIGNATURE: Norge or WCI

WHIRLPOOL: From the 50's into the early 80's, Whirlpool used essentially the same old, dependable, bullet-proof design. They are known in the parts houses as "Whirlpool belt-drive" models.

In the early 80's, Whirlpool began distributing their "Design 2000" washers (known in the parts houses as "Whirlpool direct drive" models.)

Both are covered in this book, in Chapters 3 & 4.

WHITE-WESTINGHOUSE: WCI

1-1(a) WEIRD STUFF

"SUDS SAVER" FEATURES

A *few* old machines were built with so-called "suds saver" features. They are characterized by having TWO drain hoses. One is supposed to lead to an external "suds" tank (usually a laundry tub-sink) where the wash water from a first load can be re-used for a second load. There is a suds diverter valve in the washer, and sometimes a suds return pump separate from the main washer pump.

If you have one of these washers (not likely; they're pretty rare) do yourself a favor and disconnect the suds pump and/or diverter valve. Route all pump discharge out through the drain.

Or else get a gun and shoot the bloomin' thing. They're just about impossible to get parts for.

UP-AND-DOWN AGITATOR

For a time, Frigidaire made a washer with an agitator (called a "pulsator") that moved up and down rather than rotating back and forth. They were solenoid-controlled and obviously the transmission was different, but otherwise the control systems were about the same as other washers. They're very difficult and expensive to get parts for.

1-2. BEFORE YOU START

Find yourself a good appliance parts dealer. You can find them in the Yellow Pages under the following headings:

● APPLIANCES, HOUSEHOLD, MAJOR
● APPLIANCES, PARTS AND SUPPLIES
● REFRIGERATORS, DOMESTIC
● APPLIANCES, HOUSEHOLD, REPAIR AND SERVICE

Call a few of them and ask if they are a repair service, or if they sell parts, or both. Ask them if they offer free advice with the parts they sell. (Occasionally, stores that offer parts *and* service will not want to give you advice.) Often, the parts counter men are ex-technicians who got tired of the pressure of going into peoples' houses and selling a job. They can be your best friends; however, you don't want to badger them with TOO many questions, so know your basics before you start asking questions.

Some parts houses may offer service too. Be careful! They may try to talk you out of even *trying* to fix your own washer. They'll tell you it's too complicated, then in the same breath, "guide" you to their service department. Who are you gonna believe, me or them? Not all service/parts places are this way, however. If they genuinely *try* to help you fix it yourself and you find that you can't fix the problem, they may be a really good place to look for service.

When you go into the store, have ready your make, model and serial number from the *nameplate* of the washer.

NAMEPLATE INFORMATION

The metal nameplate information is usually found in one of the places shown in Figure 1-1:

A) Along the bottom panel; on the left or right corner.

B) Inside or underneath the lid.

C) Somewhere on the back of the washer.

D) Side or top of the console

If all else fails, check the original papers that came with your washer when it was new. They should contain the model number SOMEWHERE.

If you have absolutely NO information about the washer anywhere, make sure you bring your old part to the parts store with you. Sometimes they can match an old part by looks or by part number.

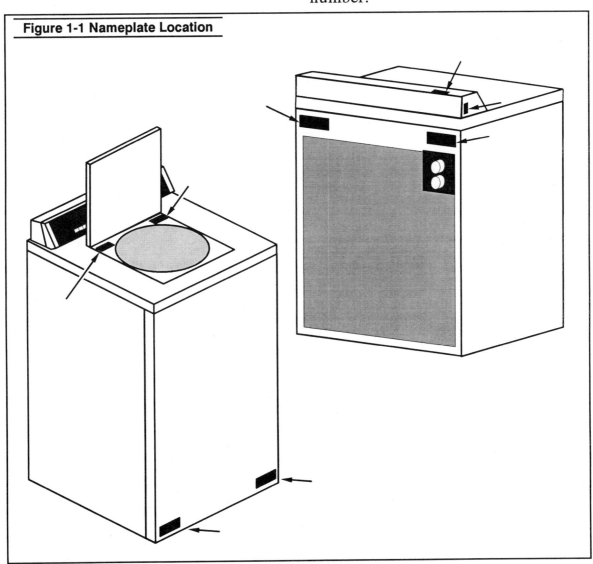

Figure 1-1 Nameplate Location

1-3. TOOLS (Figure 1-2)

The tools that you may need (depending on the diagnosis) are listed below. Some are optional. The reason for the option is explained.

For certain repairs, you will need a special tool. These are inexpensively available from your appliance parts dealer. They are listed in this book as needed.

SCREWDRIVERS: Both flat and phillips head; two or three different sizes of each. It is best to have at least a stubby, 4" and 6" sizes.

NUTDRIVERS: You will need at least a 1/4" and a 5/16" nut driver. 4" or 6" ones should suffice, but it's better to have stubbies, too.

OPEN END/BOX WRENCHES

SOCKET WRENCHES

ELECTRICAL PLIERS or STRIPPERS and DIAGONAL CUTTING PLIERS: For cutting and stripping small electrical wire.

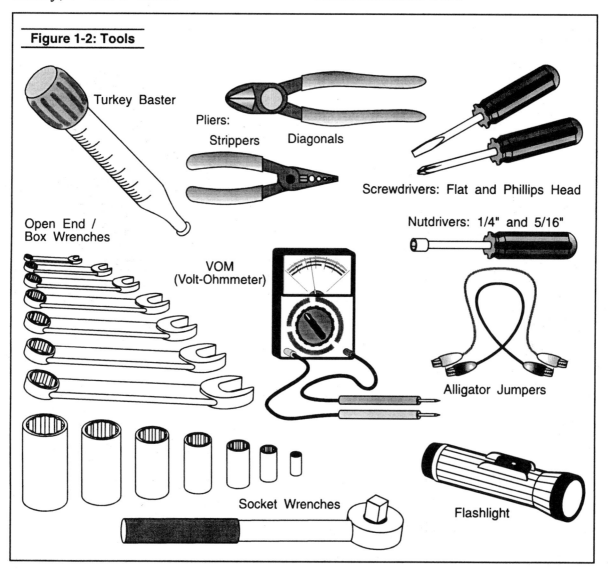

Figure 1-2: Tools

Turkey Baster

Pliers:
Strippers   Diagonals

Screwdrivers: Flat and Phillips Head

Nutdrivers: 1/4" and 5/16"

Open End /
Box Wrenches

VOM
(Volt-Ohmmeter)

Alligator Jumpers

Socket Wrenches

Flashlight

BUTT CONNECTORS, CRIMPERS, WIRE NUTS AND ELECTRICAL TAPE: For splicing small wire.

VOM(VOLT-OHM METER): For testing circuits. If you do not have one, get one. An inexpensive one will suffice, as long as it has both "A.C. Voltage" and "Resistance" (i.e. R x 1, R x 10, etc.) settings on the dial. It will do for our purposes. If you are inexperienced in using one, get an analog (pointer) type (as opposed to a digital.)

ALLIGATOR JUMPERS (sometimes called a "CHEATER" or "CHEATER WIRE"): small gauge (14-16 gauge or so) and about 12 to 18 inches long; for testing electrical circuits. Available at your local electronics store. Cost: a few bucks for 4 or 5 of them.

FLASHLIGHT: For obvious reasons.

SYRINGE TYPE TURKEY BASTER: For cleaning fill hose and fill solenoid valve strainer screens.

OPTIONAL TOOLS
(Figure 1-3)

SNAP-AROUND AMMETER: For determining if electrical components are energized. Quite useful; but a bit expensive, and there are alternate methods. If you have one, use it; otherwise, don't bother getting one.

EXTENDABLE INSPECTION MIRROR: For seeing difficult places beneath the washer and behind panels.

CORDLESS POWER SCREWDRIVER OR DRILL/DRIVER WITH MAGNETIC SCREWDRIVER AND NUTDRIVER TIPS: For pulling off panels held in place by many screws. It can save you lots of time and hassle.

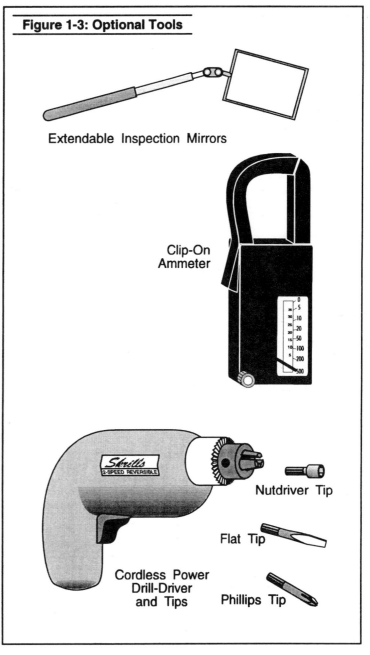

Figure 1-3: Optional Tools

Extendable Inspection Mirrors

Clip-On Ammeter

Nutdriver Tip

Flat Tip

Cordless Power Drill-Driver and Tips

Phillips Tip

1-4. HOW TO USE A VOM AND AMMETER

Many home handymen are very intimidated by electricity. It's true that diagnosing and repairing electrical circuits requires a *bit* more care than most operations, due to the danger of getting shocked. But there is no mystery or voo-

Figure 1-4: Testing Voltage

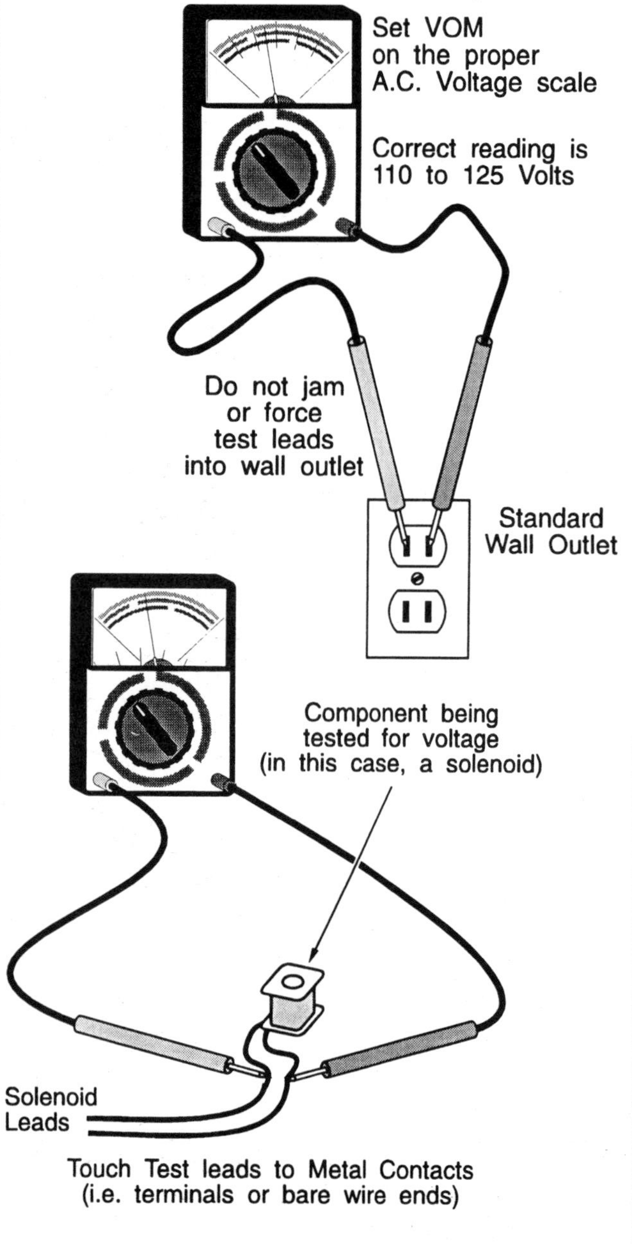

Set VOM on the proper A.C. Voltage scale

Correct reading is 110 to 125 Volts

Do not jam or force test leads into wall outlet

Standard Wall Outlet

Component being tested for voltage (in this case, a solenoid)

Solenoid Leads

Touch Test leads to Metal Contacts (i.e. terminals or bare wire ends)

doo about the things we'll be doing. Remember the rule in section 1-5 (1); while you are working on a circuit, energize the circuit only long enough to perform whatever test you're performing, then take the power back off it to perform the repair. You need not be concerned with any theory, like what an ohm is, or what a volt is. You will only need to be able to set the VOM onto the right scale, touch the test leads to the right place and read the meter.

In using the VOM (Volt-Ohm Meter) for our purposes, the two test leads are always plugged into the "+" and "-" holes on the VOM. (Some VOMs have more than two holes.)

1-4(a). TESTING VOLTAGE (Figure 1-4)

Set the dial of the VOM on the lowest VAC scale (A.C. Voltage) over 120 volts. For example, if there's a 50 setting and a 250 setting on the VAC dial, use the 250 scale, because 250 is the lowest setting over 120 volts.

Touch the two test leads to the two metal contacts of a live power source, like a wall outlet or the terminals of the motor that you're testing for voltage. (*Do not* **jam** *the test leads into a wall outlet!*) If you are getting power through the VOM, the meter will jump up and steady on a reading. You *may* have to convert the scale in your head. For example, if you're using the 250 volt dial setting and the meter has a "25" scale, simply divide by 10; 120 volts would be "12" on the meter.

1-4(b). TESTING FOR CONTINUITY (Figure 1-5)

Don't let the word "continuity" scare you. It's derived from the word "continuous." In an electrical circuit, electricity has to flow *from* a power source back *to* that power source. If there is any break in the circuit, it is not continuous, and it has no continuity. "Good" continuity means that there is no break in the circuit.

For example, if you were testing a solenoid to see if it was burned out, you would try putting a small amount of power through the solenoid. If it was burned out, there would be a break in the circuit, the electricity wouldn't flow, and your meter would show no continuity.

That is what the resistance part of your VOM does; it provides a small electrical current (using batteries within the VOM) and measures how fast the current is flowing. For our purposes, it doesn't matter how *fast* the current is flowing; only that there *is* current flow.

To use your VOM to test continuity, set the dial on (resistance) R x 1, or whatever the lowest setting is. Touch the metal parts of the test leads together and read the meter. It should peg the meter all the way on the right side of the scale, towards "0" on the meter's "resistance" scale. If the meter does not read zero resistance, adjust the thumbwheel on the front of the VOM until it *does* read zero. If you cannot get the meter to read zero, the battery in the VOM is low; replace it.

If you are testing, say, a solenoid, first make sure that the solenoid leads are not connected to anything, especially a power source. If the solenoid's leads are still connected to something, you may get a reading through that something. If there is still live power on the item you're testing for continuity, you will burn out your VOM instantly and possibly shock yourself.

Touch the two test leads to the two bare wire ends or terminals of the solenoid. You can touch the ends of the

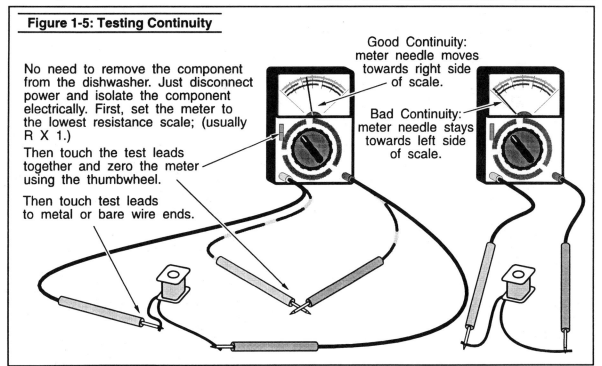

Figure 1-5: Testing Continuity

No need to remove the component from the dishwasher. Just disconnect power and isolate the component electrically. First, set the meter to the lowest resistance scale; (usually R X 1.)

Then touch the test leads together and zero the meter using the thumbwheel.

Then touch test leads to metal or bare wire ends.

Good Continuity: meter needle moves towards right side of scale.

Bad Continuity: meter needle stays towards left side of scale.

wires and test leads with your hands if necessary to get better contact. The voltage that the VOM batteries put out is very low, and you will not be shocked. If there is NO continuity, the meter won't move. If there is GOOD continuity, the meter will move toward the right side of the scale and steady on a reading. This is the resistance reading and it doesn't concern us; we only care that we show good continuity. If the meter moves only very little and stays towards the left side of the scale, that's BAD continuity; the solenoid is no good.

If you are testing a switch, you will show little or no resistance (good continuity) when the switch is closed, and NO continuity when the switch is open. If you do not, the switch is bad.

1-4(c). AMMETERS

Ammeters are a little bit more complex to explain without going into a lot of electrical theory. If you own an ammeter, you probably already know how to use it.

If you don't, don't get one. Ammeters are expensive. And for *our* purposes,

there are other ways to determine what an ammeter tests for. If you don't own one, skip this section.

For our purposes, ammeters are simply a way of testing for continuity without having to cut into the system or to disconnect power from whatever it is we're testing.

Ammeters measure the current in amps flowing through a wire. The greater the current that's flowing *through* a wire, the greater the density of the magnetic field, or *flux*, it produces *around* the wire. The ammeter simply measures the density of this flux, and thus the amount of current, flowing through the wire. To determine continuity, for our purposes, we can simply isolate the component that we're testing (so we do not accidentally measure the current going through any other components) and see if there's *any* current flow.

To use your ammeter, first make sure that it's on an appropriate scale (0 to 10 or 20 amps will do). Isolate a wire leading directly to the component you're testing. Put the ammeter loop around that wire and read the meter. (Figure 1-6)

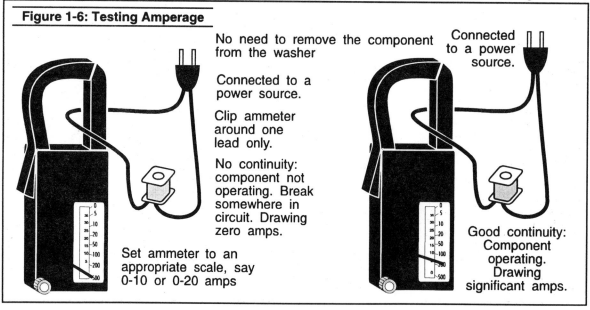

Figure 1-6: Testing Amperage

No need to remove the component from the washer

Connected to a power source.

Clip ammeter around one lead only.

No continuity: component not operating. Break somewhere in circuit. Drawing zero amps.

Set ammeter to an appropriate scale, say 0-10 or 0-20 amps

Connected to a power source.

Good continuity: Component operating. Drawing significant amps.

1-5. BASIC REPAIR AND SAFETY PRECAUTIONS

1) Always de-energize (pull the plug or trip the breaker on) any washer that you're disassembling. If you need to re-energize the washer to perform a test, make sure any bare wires or terminals are taped or insulated. Energize the unit only long enough to perform whatever test you're performing, then disconnect the power again.

2) If the manual advocates replacing the part, REPLACE IT!! You might find, say, a solenoid that has jammed for no apparent reason. Sometimes you can clean it out and lubricate it, and get it going again. The key words here are *apparent reason*. There is a reason that it stopped--you can bet on it--and if you get it going and re-install it, you are running a very high risk that it will stop again. If *that* happens, you will have to start re-pairing your washer *all* over again. It may only act up when it is hot, or it may be bent slightly...there are a hundred different "what if's." Very few of the parts mentioned in this book will cost you over ten or twenty dollars. Replace the part.

3) To work underneath the washer sometimes requires leaning the washer back against the wall at a 30- to 45-degree angle. When you do, always block up one corner of the washer as shown in Figure 1-7. NEVER DO THIS ALONE! Al-ways have someone standing by to help you while you work beneath the washer, in case it comes down on you.

4) If you must lay the washer over on its side, front or back, first make sure that you are not going to break anything off, such as a drain hose or fill valve. Lay an old blanket on the floor to protect the floor and the finish of the washer. And for goodness' sake, make sure you drain the thing completely first!

5) Always replace the green (ground) leads when you remove an electrical component. They're there for a reason. And NEVER EVER remove the third (ground) prong in the main power plug!

6) When opening the washer cabinet or console, remember that the sheet metal parts are have very sharp edges. Wear gloves, and be careful not to cut your hands!

Figure 1-7: Leaning the Washer Against the Wall

To access belts or other parts underneath the washer:

Lean the washer against the wall at a 30 to 45 degree angle and block up the corner with a wood block

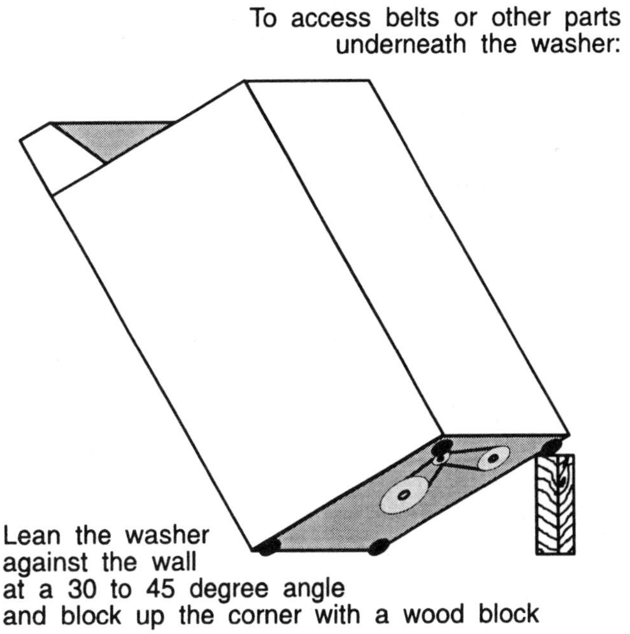

CAUTION: ALWAYS HAVE A HELPER STANDING BY IN CASE THE WASHER STARTS TO COME DOWN ON YOU!!!

1-6. TIPS & TRICKS

Following are a few hard-earned pearls of wisdom:

1) When testing for your power supply from a wall outlet, plug in a small appliance such as a shaver or blow dryer. If you're not getting full power out of the outlet, you'll know it right away.

2) If you just can't get that agitator unstuck, your appliance parts dealer has a device called an Agi-Tamer for just such an occurrence.

3) If you need to drain the tub (usually because your pump isn't pumping out) most folks try to bail it out. That's a wet, messy, yucky job, and not very thorough.

Try this instead: use your garden hose as a siphon.

However, when you do, another problem arises: did you ever try to suck a charge of wash water through a fifty-foot garden hose? If you can, you've got one heckuva set of lungs. And what happens when that nice, week-old dirty wash water reaches your mouth?

You guessed it: there's a better way.

What's the point in sucking the water through the hose? To get rid of the air in it, right? Well, instead of using *lung suction* to do that, let's use *house pressure*.

Leave your garden hose connected to the faucet, and put the other end of it in the washer tub. Turn the faucet on for a few seconds, until it stops bubbling in the tub. The air is gone now, right?

Kink the garden hose so you don't lose the water charge, and disconnect it from the faucet. When you're sure the faucet end of the hose is lower than the bottom of the washer tub, release the kink in the hose. The tub will drain, almost completely, in just a few minutes. No muss, no fuss.

Chapter 2

PROBLEMS COMMON TO ALL BRANDS

Washing machine designs vary widely, but there are *some* things that *all* washers have in common. For example, all washers have an electric motor. All washers have both spin and agitate cycles. And since both cycles are driven by the same electric motor, all washers have some sort of mechanism to change between the two.

All washers must also have a way of filling the tub with wash water and a way of draining out used wash water. And incidental to this, all washers must have a way of controlling water level in the tub, to prevent spillage by overfill or by centrifugal force during the spin cycle.

All washers must (by law) have a mechanism that brakes the spinning basket at the end of the spin cycle.

And last but not least, all washers must have a timer that controls and coordinates the start, stop and duration of the various cycles.

2-1 CYCLES

FILL CYCLE

During the FILL cycle, a solenoid-operated water mixing valve opens and allows hot or cold water (or both) to enter the tub. There is no pump operating at this time; the tub fills strictly from house pressure. Similarly, there is no heater in your washer; the heat comes from the hot water heater in your home.

When the water in the tub reaches a certain level, the water solenoid valve closes. Water level is sensed either by a pressure switch or, in some older models, a float switch or waterweight switch.

WASH/RINSE (AGITATION) CYCLE

After the water valve closes, an electric motor starts which drives the transmission, usually through a belt, and in some cases through a clutch arrangement, too. The transmission converts the rotary motion of the motor to the back-and-forth motion of the agitator. A driveshaft extends from the top of the transmission to the agitator, where it is connected to the agitator, usually by a spline. (See Figure G-1.)

Agitation will continue for a certain amount of time, which is controlled by the timer. During agitation, some washers use their pump to circulate water, sucking it from the bottom of the tub and pumping it to the top of the tub. The pump is driven by the same electric motor.

Also during the agitation cycle, bleach or softener may be automatically added. This is usually done by a solenoid valve that allows some of the recirculated water to flush out the bleach or softener dispenser. In some models there is no water circulation involved; the solenoid simply opens a valve or door that lets the dispenser contents drop into the wash water. The timer tells this solenoid valve when to open.

Figure G-1: Typical Drive Train

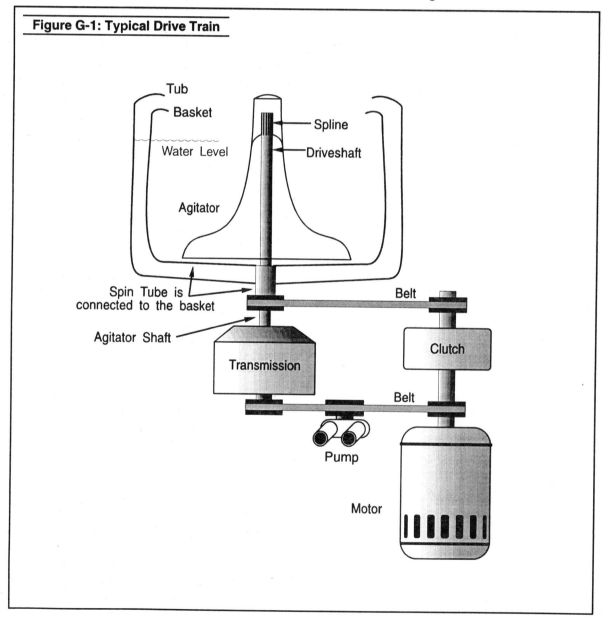

SPIN AND DRAIN CYCLES

After agitation comes a drain cycle, sometimes combined with a spin cycle. During the drain cycle, the pump sucks water from the tub and sends it down the drain. During the spin cycle, the same motor that drove the agitator now drives a spin tube which is concentric with the agitator shaft. (See Figure G-1) The spin tube spins the basket, slinging excess water out of the clothes by centrifugal force. There is a clutch arrangement which allows the basket to come up to speed slowly. This prevents a heavy load from being thrown onto the motor suddenly. It also allows a "pre-pump" action; the water has a chance to drain out of the tub before the basket gets up to speed, preventing the water from overflowing the edge of the tub by centrifugal force.

Some brands have a partial drain cycle only, then refill and agitate again. Some start spinning and draining at the same time. Some only drain until the water reaches a certain level, then start spinning. Most brands have lid switches that prevent the basket from spinning when the lid is open. Some brands have a lid lock that prevents you from opening the lid when the basket is spinning.

At the end of the spin cycle, or whenever the lid is lifted, most models have a braking arrangement that stops the tub from spinning. This helps to prevent people from accidently sticking their hands into a spinning basket.

CAUTION: NEVER BYPASS THE LID SWITCH, EXCEPT FOR TEST PURPOSES. IF IT IS DEFECTIVE, INSTALL A NEW ONE. THEY ARE THERE FOR A REASON.

2-2 FILL SYSTEM

The basic components of the fill system are the hoses, the fill valve, and the pressure or float switch.

The fill valve (Figure G-2) is simply a solenoid valve that opens when activated and allows hot and/or cold water to flow into the tub. Most modern washers use dual solenoid valves, which have both hot and cold solenoids in one valve body. When *warm* water is desired, both valves open to mix hot and cold.

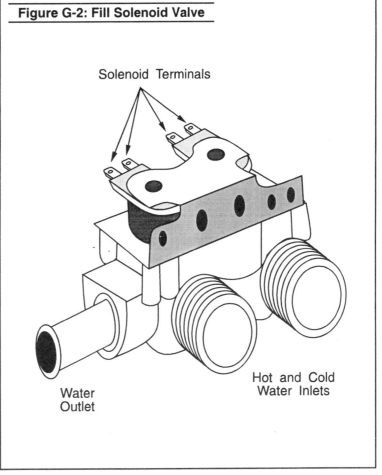

Figure G-2: Fill Solenoid Valve

Solenoid Terminals

Water Outlet

Hot and Cold Water Inlets

When the water in the tub reaches the desired level, the pressure or float switch closes the circuit to the fill valve. Float switches are uncommon; you'll find them only in older washers. A diaphragm-type pressure switch is more common. Typical float and pressure switches are shown in Figure G-3. A few old washers used a pressure switch mounted on the BOTTOM of the tub; these are known as water weight switches. They are rare.

DIAGNOSIS

If your washer is not filling properly, or is overflowing, there could be several reasons.

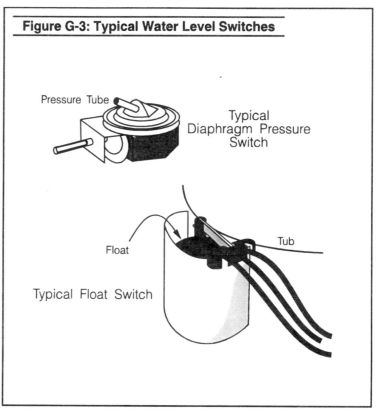

Figure G-3: Typical Water Level Switches

Pressure Tube

Typical Diaphragm Pressure Switch

Float

Tub

Typical Float Switch

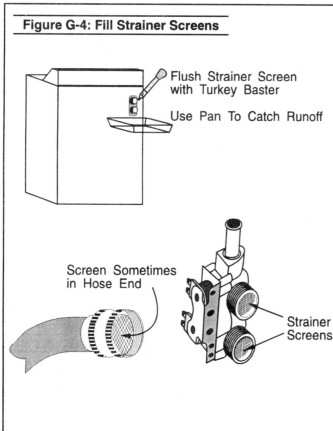

Figure G-4: Fill Strainer Screens

Flush Strainer Screen with Turkey Baster

Use Pan To Catch Runoff

Screen Sometimes in Hose End

Strainer Screens

SLOW OR NO FILL, OR WATER TOO HOT OR TOO COLD

If your washer is filling very slowly or not at all, or the water temperature is always too hot or too cold, check the fill hose and valve strainers. These are little strainers placed in the fill hose and/ or water valve to prevent rust and scale from your house's piping system from getting into the water valve. The strainers can get clogged up over time and prevent water flow.

Shut off the water valves and remove the hoses. Look into the both ends of each hose and into the water valve mounted on the washer. In at least one of the three places you should see a strainer screen. (Figure G-4) If it is clogged, you can try cleaning it out with a toothbrush and/or a turkey baster. If you cannot clean the screen sufficiently, you may need to replace it. In some instances, the screen is non-removable, and you will need to replace the hose or valve. Neither is very expensive.

When re-installing the hoses, always use new hose washers. Also, take care not to overtighten the hose on the plastic threads of the solenoid valve; tighten just enough to stop it from leaking. If there is any question about the water-tight integrity of the hose, replace it. A hose costs a lot less than a new floor or carpeting, which is what you'll be buying if it breaks while you're not home.

If the strainers look O.K., set your temperature control to "warm" and set your timer in the fill cycle. Raise the lid of the washer and depress any lid switch with a pen or screwdriver. Feel the water entering the washer. If it is too hot or too cold, or if no water is coming out at all,

test for voltage across each solenoid coil of the water valve as shown in figure G-5. It should read 110 to 125 volts.

If so, you're getting power to your valve, but it's not opening. Replace the valve.

If you're not getting power to the valve, refer to the wiring diagram for your machine (see section 2-5) and trace the source of the interruption. Sometimes it's a broken wire, but more commonly, there will be a problem with the water level switch, timer, lid switch, or temperature switch. Replace the defective switch.

CAUTION: On some brands, you must raise the top of the cabinet to get to the solenoid valve. If your washer has a mercury-tube type lid switch, raising the top of the cabinet may have the same effect on the lid switch as raising the lid. Your washer may not fill or cycle. You will need to jumper the mercury switch to perform any tests when the cabinet top is raised.

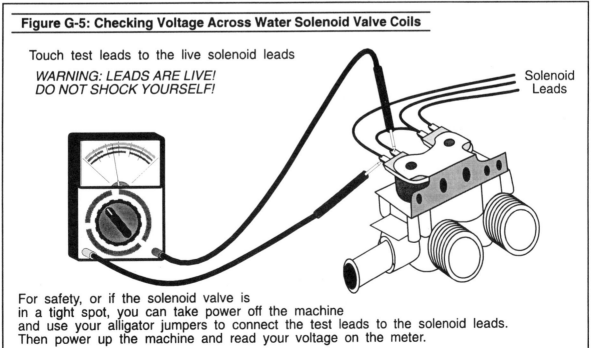

Figure G-5: Checking Voltage Across Water Solenoid Valve Coils

Touch test leads to the live solenoid leads
WARNING: LEADS ARE LIVE!
DO NOT SHOCK YOURSELF!

Solenoid Leads

For safety, or if the solenoid valve is in a tight spot, you can take power off the machine and use your alligator jumpers to connect the test leads to the solenoid leads. Then power up the machine and read your voltage on the meter.

OVERFILL

As the tub fills, water pressure increases at the bottom of the tub. This pressure is transmitted to the diaphragm in the water level switch by a rubber or plastic tube. (Figure G-6) When the tub reaches the right level, the diaphragm trips the switch, closing the solenoid valve and starting the agitate cycle.

If the tube or diaphragm is leaking in any way, the water level switch will not sense any pressure, and thus will not shut off the water flow, so the tub will overflow.

CAUTION: Whenever you remove the tube from the switch, or insert the tube onto the switch, there cannot be any water in the tub or tube. Before you insert the tube onto the switch, blow into the tube first, to clear it of any water that might have gotten in it. ANY WATER REMAINING IN THE TUBE WILL CAUSE YOUR WASHER TO OVERFLOW!

Also test the water level switch electrically, as described in section 2-5(b).

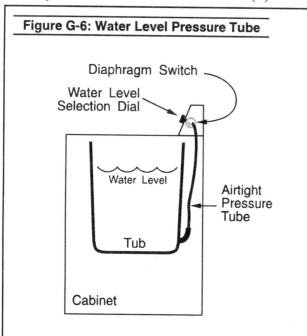

Figure G-6: Water Level Pressure Tube

Diaphragm Switch

Water Level Selection Dial

Water Level

Airtight Pressure Tube

Tub

Cabinet

DOES NOT STOP FILLING, AND/OR WATER LEVEL KEEPS GOING DOWN

If the house washer drain starts backing up, you get a rooter and clear the drain, right? But *some* people would just seal it up so it couldn't overflow, instead of clearing the drain, as they should. (Now, *WE* wouldn't do that, would we, folks?)

But that air break between the washer's drain hose and the house's drain pipe is important. If there is no air break, and the drain system fills with water, it can actually start siphoning water right through the pump and down the drain. Depending on how bad the drain is backing up, the washer might never fill completely; the solenoid valve will just stay open and water will just keep siphoning straight out the drain. Or, if the drain is a little more clogged and the water is flowing more slowly, the washer might fill and start agitating, but stop agitating after a few minutes and fill some more. This fill-agitate-fill-agitate cycle will continue for as long as the agitate cycle lasts. And since the power to the timer motor is being interrupted, the wash and rinse cycles may seem unusually long.

There is a solution, even if you don't want to root out the drain blockage as you should. Your appliance parts dealer has a drain line vacuum break valve, available for just a few bucks. (Figure G-7) You can cut into your drain line and install one of these vacuum breaks pretty easily.

When the drain line is under pressure, (like when the pump is pumping out) the flapper valve closes and no leakage occurs. When the drain line is under a vacuum (like when the drain is trying to siphon it) the flapper valve opens and air is allowed into the drain line, breaking the siphoning action.

2-3 PUMP; DRAIN AND RECIRCULATION SYSTEMS

The pump can perform several functions. In all washers, it is used to pump water out of the tub at the end of an agitate or soak cycle. In some washers, it also circulates water during the agitate cycle. It may also provide flush water for a bleach or softener dispenser. Therefore, the pump *may* be required to pump in two different directions or more during a cycle.

Some brands and/or models accomplish this by using two different pump impellers in one body; the pump body will have two inlets and two outlets. Others use a solenoid-activated butterfly valve in the pump body to re-direct the waterflow. Still others use a direct-reversing pump; the motor driving the pump turns in the opposite direction, and the pump pumps in the opposite direction.

DIAGNOSIS

Sometimes the most obvious answers are the first ones overlooked. If the tub isn't draining, first check the drain system. Check the drain hose to make sure it isn't kinked. Also check any lint filter that may be installed. On some Whirlpool/Kenmore models, there is also a side-check valve at the tub outlet that can get clogged.

There aren't too many things that can go wrong with a pump. The pump bearings can seize, stopping it from turning. The pump can be jammed by socks or other small items. The impeller blades can break off due to junk entering the pump; if this happens, the pump may seize up, or it may just stop pumping. The usual solution is to replace the pump, although pumps in a few models are rebuildable.

But the *symptoms* of a pump failure are something else altogether. If the pump locks up, and the motor is still trying to turn it, *something's* gotta give. If the pump is belt-driven (as it is in many washers) the pulley driving the pump may shear off, or the belt may break. The belt may ride over the locked pulley, or the motor pulley will continue turning under the belt; this will burn the belt and possibly break it. There may even be enough tension on the belt to stop the motor from turning.

The symptoms can be confusing. For example, a common complaint about a Whirlpool belt-drive washer is that it isn't spinning, accompanied by a strong burning smell. The problem is almost always a pump that's locked up. The washer

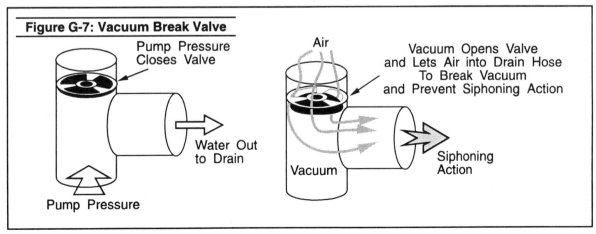

Figure G-7: Vacuum Break Valve

Pump Pressure Closes Valve

Water Out to Drain

Pump Pressure

Air

Vacuum Opens Valve and Lets Air into Drain Hose To Break Vacuum and Prevent Siphoning Action

Siphoning Action

Vacuum

doesn't enter the spin cycle because the spin is interlocked with the drain cycle. This means that the basket won't start spinning until the water is partially drained. The burning smell comes from the rubber belt, which is riding over the motor pulley or locked pump pulley.

NOTE: If you EVER find a broken belt, check for a locked pump, transmission or other pulley before replacing the belt.

If you suspect that something is jamming the pump, drain the tub and pull the hoses off the pump. Look into the hoses and the pump and pull out whatever is jamming it. If you can't see anything jamming the pump, feel around the inside of the pump inlets and outlets with a pair of needlenose pliers. If all else fails, and you still can't find the jam, pull the pump out of the machine and check it.

For specific information about pump replacement or service, see the chapter about *your* brand.

2-4 TRANSMISSION AND DRIVE TRAIN

Besides driving the pump, the motor has two main functions: to spin the basket and reciprocate the agitator. One motor is used to do both.

Within the transmission there is typically a crank gear and connecting rod arrangement to provide the reciprocating motion to the agitator. However, some designs use a differential gear, slider, eccentric, or other design.

The spin motion comes directly from the rotary motion of the motor, through some clutch arrangement. Usually there is some kind of reduction arrangement in the belt or gearing.

There must also be some mechanism to change between spin and agitate. There are two ways that this is most commonly done.

Many washer designs use solenoids to engage and disengage clutches and transmissions. The solenoid engages a clutch to turn the basket in the spin cycle. For the agitate cycle, a solenoid (sometimes the same one) disengages the clutch and engages the transmission. For specific information see the chapter about *your* brand.

Many washer designs use a direct-reversing motor. When the motor turns one way, a mechanical arrangement such as a helical shaft, centrifugal clutch or torsion spring engages and spins the basket. When the motor reverses, the brake locks the basket and the transmission engages, so the agitator agitates.

The basket braking arrangement is often a part of the clutch arrangement. Braking is usually "fail-safe""that is, if the solenoid or mechanical arrangement that engages the spin mode fails, the brake will stop the basket automatically.

For specific information about YOUR washer's drive train, see the chapter pertaining to your brand.

2-4(a) BELTS

Look closely at the surface of the belt. If you see any of the problems shown in figure G-8, replace it.

Broken or worn out belts are a common problem. See the chapter on *your* brand for specific details about changing the belt(s) on your model. If you **EVER** find a broken belt, check for a locked pump, transmission or other pulley before replacing the belt.

2-4(b) AGITATOR

If your washer is agitating weakly or not at all, the splines that connect it to the driveshaft may be stripped. It's a fairly common problem. Remove the agitator as described in the chapter specific to your washer. If the shaft *is* rotating but the agitator is *not*, replace the agitator or spline insert.

2-4(c) TRANSMISSIONS

Transmissions in general are pretty bullet-proof, and rarely experience problems beyond a little oil loss. There are exceptions; see the chapter pertaining to your washer.

If your transmission is leaking oil badly, you basically have two options: replace the transmission now, or keep running it until it runs out of oil and dies. Nobody I know of rebuilds transmissions themselves any more. It is far quicker and easier to just replace it with a rebuilt. See the chapter about your brand for replacement details.

Occasionally, something will break inside the casing and lock the transmission, or prohibit its operation in one mode or another.

The symptoms may be similar to a locked pump; stalled motor, burning belt, etc.

To diagnose this, first unplug your washer. Try turning the motor by hand, or pull the belt so everything rotates. *Be careful you don't pinch your fingers between the belt and pulley!* Check to see that every pulley that the belt rides is rotating. It should be pretty stiff, but if you can't turn it at all, something is locked up. Disengage the drive system (remove the belt, etc.) Try to turn the transmission drive pulley with your hand. Also check the movement of the pump, and any tensioner or idler pulley that may be present.

Do not try to rebuild your own transmission. Typically, rebuilding requires special tools that drive the cost above that of buying a rebuilt transmission. Rebuilt trannies for the more popular models are inexpensively available from your parts dealer, and usually kept in stock.

There are a few very poor designs out there that are not worth fixing; you are better off scrapping the washer. Due to some parts business politics, I can't mention brand names in this book, but your parts dealer will probably be happy to privately let you know which ones they are.

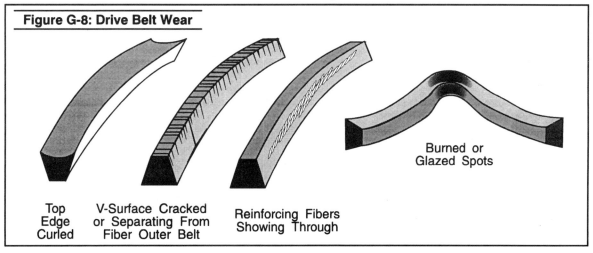

Figure G-8: Drive Belt Wear

Top Edge Curled

V-Surface Cracked or Separating From Fiber Outer Belt

Reinforcing Fibers Showing Through

Burned or Glazed Spots

2-5 TESTING ELECTRICAL COMPONENTS

Sometimes you need to read a wiring diagram, to make sure you are not forgetting to check something. Sometimes you just need to find out what color wire to look for to test a component. It is ESPECIALLY important in diagnosing a bad timer.

If you already know how to read a wiring diagram, you can skip this section. If you're one of those folks who's a bit timid around electricity, all I can say is read on, and don't be too nervous. It will come to you. You learned how to use a VOM in Chapter 1, right?

Look at figure G-9. The symbol used to represent each component is pretty universal, and each component should be labelled clearly on your diagram.

A few notes about reading a wiring diagram:

Notice that in some parts of the diagram, the lines are thicker than in other parts. The wiring and switches that are shown as thick lines are *inside* of the timer.

The small circles all over the diagram are terminals. These are places where you can disconnect the wire from the component for testing purposes.

If you see dotted or shaded lines around a group of wires, this is a switch assembly; for example, a water level, water temperature or motor speed switch assembly; it may also be the timer, but whatever it is, it should

be clearly marked on the diagram. Any wiring enclosed by a shaded or dotted box is internal to a switch assembly and must be tested as described in sections 2-5(c) and 2-5(d).

Switches may be numbered on the diagram, but that number will *not* be found on the switch. Those numbers are there to help you follow the timer sequencing chart. Don't worry about the timer sequencing chart. We are only concerned to see *if* the switch is opening and closing. We'll let the design engineers worry about exactly *when* it opens and closes.

To find (and test) a switch with a certain number, look for the color of the wires leading to the switch.

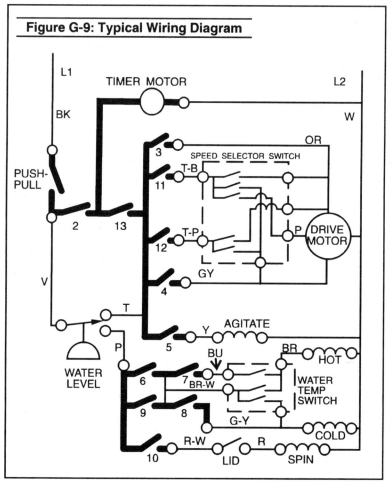

Figure G-9: Typical Wiring Diagram

Wire colors are abbreviated; for example, BU means blue, BL or B means black, V means violet, T means tan. If you see a wire color with a dash or a slash, that means —— with a —— stripe. For example, OR-W means orange with a white stripe; G/P means green with a pink stripe.

NOTE: Green wires are ground wires and MUST be re-connected when removed.

Remember that for something to be energized, it must make a complete electrical circuit. You must be able to trace the path that the electricity will take, FROM the wall outlet back TO the wall outlet. This includes not only the component that you suspect, but all switches leading to it. In Figure G-9(a), L1 and L2 are the main power leads; they go directly to your wall plug.

Let's say you need to check out why the spin solenoid is not working. Following the gray-shaded circuit in figure G-9(a), the electricity flows through the black wire (L1) to the push-pull switch. This switch is located inside of the timer (you know this because it is drawn with thick lines) and it must be closed. The power then goes through the violet wire to the water level switch (which must have a LOW water level,) then through the pink wire back into the timer. Inside the timer, it goes through switch number 10. It then comes out of the timer in a red wire with a white

stripe (R-W) that leads to the lid switch (which must be closed.) From the lid switch, it goes through a red wire to the spin solenoid. Finally it leaves the spin solenoid in a white wire, which leads back to the main power cord (L2).

If you're not sure whether a certain switch or component is a part of the circuit you're diagnosing, *assume* that it is and test it. For example, switches 3,4,11 & 12 all lead to the motor circuit. If you have a motor problem that you think you've traced to the timer, don't bother trying to figure out which switch goes to which part of the motor. Test all four; if any of the four switches is bad, you will need to replace the whole timer, anyway.

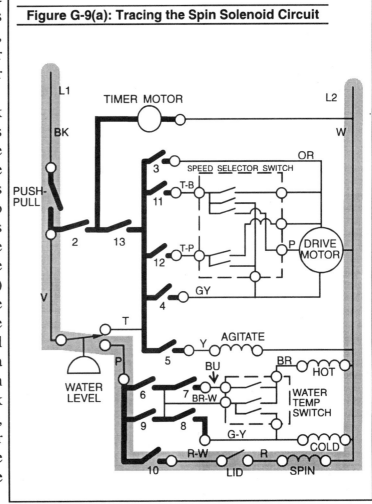

Figure G-9(a): Tracing the Spin Solenoid Circuit

To test for the break in the circuit, simply isolate each part of the system (remove the wires from the terminals) and test for continuity. For example, to test the spin solenoid in our example, pull the red and white wires off the spin solenoid and test continuity across the solenoid terminals as described in section 2-5(a).

The push-pull switch, and switch number 10 are shown in bold lines, so they are inside the timer. Looking at the diagram, the push-pull switch controls a lot of other things besides the spin solenoid. Since those things are working O.K., we know that the push-pull switch can't be the problem.

For now, let's ignore switch number 10. (Remember: the timer is the *last* thing you should check; see section 2-5(c).)

That leaves the water level switch, the lid switch, the spin solenoid itself, and the wiring.

Nine times out of ten, a component has gone bad. Test those first. Take power off the machine and check each switch and/or solenoid in the circuit as described in sections 2-5 (a) thru (e).

To check for a wire break, you would pull each end of a wire off the component and test for continuity through it. You may need to use jumpers to extend the wire; for example, if one end of the wire is in the control console and the other end in underneath the machine. If there is no continuity, there is a break in the wire! It will then be up to you to figure out exactly where that break is; there is no magic way. If you have a broken wire, look along the length of the wire for pinching or chafing. If there is a place where the wires move (like near the wigwag of a belt-driven Whirlpool/Kenmore,) check there first. Even if the insulation is O.K., the wire may be broken inside.

INTERLOCKS

Certain safety mechanisms are installed on almost every washer that can lead you to a misdiagnosis if you forget about them.

For example, a Whirlpool washer will pump out water if the lid is open, but it won't spin. So you've just replaced the pump, and you're standing there with the lid open, admiring how well it's pumping out, when you notice it still isn't spinning. You dive right back into the back of the washer, trying to figure out what you forgot to replace...and the only problem is that the lid is up. Don't laugh; I'd hate to admit to you how many times *I've* done it.

When diagnosing an electrical problem, there are many interlocks in the system that you need to check. (See section 2-7 below.) For example, if your basket won't spin at all, you will check all the obvious stuff (lid switch, spin clutch solenoid, transmission, etc.) But will you think to check the imbalance switch? If it fails, it will have the same effect as a failed lid switch. When tracing an electrical problem, check your wiring diagram to see if there may be any forgotten switches in the malfunctioning system.

Here are a few of the more common safety interlock mechanisms to watch out for:

LID SWITCH: Mentioned above, it prevents the basket from spinning while the washer lid is open. In some designs, it also prevents the tub from filling or the agitator from agitating while the lid is open. See the note about mercury lid switches in section 2-2.

IMBALANCE INTERLOCK: If the washer has detected a substantial imbalance in the load during the spin cycle, the motor will stop. Usually a buzzer will sound. To reset this interlock, the lid must be opened and closed or the timer turned off and back on. (Presumably, you will redistribute the clothes, but it is not necessary to reset the interlock.)

WATER LEVEL INTERLOCK: On some washers, the basket will not start spinning until the water is nearly pumped out of the tub. The start of the spin cycle is dependent on the pump pumping out water and the water level switch sensing that the water level is low enough.

CAUTION: NEVER BYPASS A SAFETY INTERLOCK. THEY ARE THERE FOR A REASON.

2-5(a) SWITCHES AND SOLENOIDS

Testing switches and solenoids is pretty straightforward. Take all wires off the component and test resistance across it.

Switches should show good continuity when closed and no continuity when open.

Solenoids should show SOME resistance, but continuity should be good. If a solenoid shows no continuity, there's a break somewhere in the windings. If it shows no resistance, it's shorted.

2-5(b) WATER LEVEL SWITCHES

Water level diaphragm switches are usually shown on a wiring diagram by the symbol in figure G-10. The numbering or lettering of the terminals may differ, but basically all switches are tested the same way.

To test the switch, first fill the tub to the highest water level. Unplug the machine and set the water level switch on the lowest water level setting. Remove the three leads from the switch. Label the wires to make sure you get them back on the proper terminals.

In the example shown in figure G-10, a check for continuity should show the following:

TUB FULL: No continuity from V to P, continuity from V to T.

Re-attach the wires, plug in the machine and set the timer on "spin" or "drain." When the tub is pumped dry, stop the spin cycle and unplug the washer. Remove the wires from the water level switch and test continuity again. With an empty tub, the continuity should be reversed:

TUB EMPTY: Continuity from V to P, no continuity from V to T.

If you do not get these readings, the water level switch is bad, or there's a leak in the air pressure tube leading to it (as described in section 2-2.) Replace the switch or tube.

The labelling of the three water level switch leads is different in just about every brand, but the switch is tested in the same way. See the chapter about your brand for details about the labelling of the switch leads.

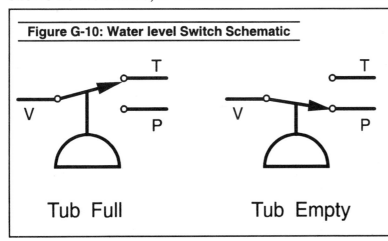

Figure G-10: Water level Switch Schematic

Tub Full   Tub Empty

2-5(c) TIMERS

The timer is the brain of the washer. It controls everything in the cycle. In addition to telling the motor when and which way to run, it tells any clutch solenoids when to engage, the fill valve when to open, dispenser solenoids when to open, etc.

The timer is nothing more than a motor that drives a set of cams which open and close switches. Yet it is one of the most expensive parts in your washer, so don't be too quick to diagnose it as the problem. Usually the FIRST thing a layman looks at is the timer; it should be the LAST. And don't forget that timers are electrical parts, which are usually non-returnable. If you buy one, and it turns out *not* to be the problem, you've just wasted the money.

In a wiring diagram, the timer may appear in two different ways (Figure G-11). The wiring and switches that are inside the timer will either be drawn with dark lines, or there will be a shaded or dotted line drawn around the timer's internal wiring and switches.

DIAGNOSIS

If the timer is not advancing, well, that's pretty obvious. Replace the timer or timer drive motor, or have it rebuilt as described below.

Timers can be difficult to diagnose. The easiest way is to go through everything else in the system that's malfunctioning. If none of the other components are bad, then it may be the timer.

Remember that a timer is simply a set of on-off switches. The switches are turned off and on by a cam, which is driven by the timer motor. Timer wires are color-coded or number-coded.

Let's say you've got a spin solenoid problem that you think you've traced to your timer. First unplug the machine. Look at your wiring diagram and see which internal timer switch feeds the spin solenoid. (See figure G-12) In this case, the pink colored wire and the red colored wire with a white stripe lead to switch #10 inside the timer. REMOVE those wires from the timer and touch the test

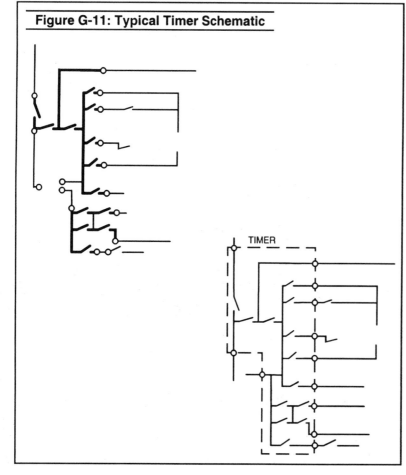

Figure G-11: Typical Timer Schematic

TIMER

leads to those terminals. Make sure the timer is in the "on" position and slowly turn the timer all the way through a full cycle. (On some timers, you cannot turn the dial while it is on. Whirlpool Direct Drive models (chapter 4) are this way. You must simply test the timer one click at a time. Be patient!)

You should see continuity make and break at least once in the cycle; usually many times. If it doesn't, the internal contacts are bad; replace the timer.

A *special* timer problem occurs only in machines with direct-reversing motors. The Whirlpool Direct-Drive models (Chapter 4) are prone to this confusing problem, though it's not too terribly common. The symptoms are that when you open the lid at the end of the cycle, the tub hasn't drained. You hear the motor running throughout the cycle, but it doesn't spin or drain; you may also notice that you hear it *agitating* when it's supposed to be *spinning*.

For the motor to reverse, the timer must interrupt power to it for a moment. When the timer gets worn, this simply doesn't happen. The motor doesn't get a chance to start in the opposite direction, so it continues to run in the same direction (agitate) until something interrupts the circuit and stops the motor. Like *you*, lifting the lid. You can see how the symptoms might appear to be intermittent and a bit confusing. The solution: replace the timer.

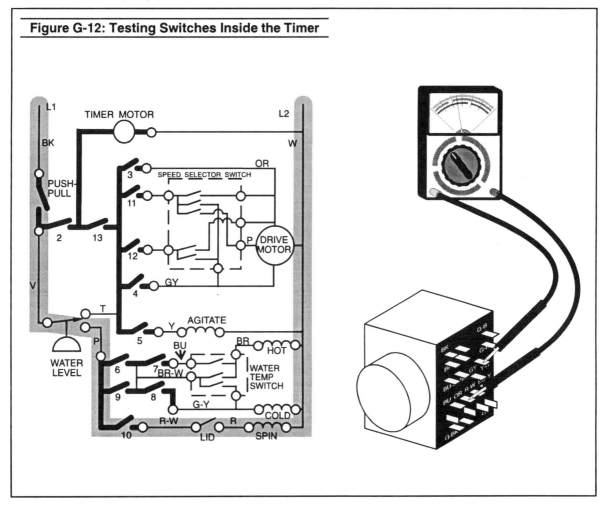

Figure G-12: Testing Switches Inside the Timer

In general, timers cannot be rebuilt by the novice. Check with your parts dealer; if it *can* be rebuilt, he'll get it done for you. If it's a common one, your parts dealer may even have a rebuilt one in stock.

For the most part, if your timer is acting up, you need to replace it. To replace, mark the wires or note the color codes written on the timer. If you need to, you can draw a picture of the terminal arrangement and wire colors. If possible, change over the timer wires one-by-one; it can be easier. If there are any special wiring changes, they will be explained in instructions that come with the new timer.

2-5(d) SPEED SELECTOR AND WATER TEMPERATURE SWITCHES

The internal wiring for these switches is almost always shown with a shaded or dotted box around them (Figure G-13.)

The lettering inside the box will tell you what terminals to test. For example, with the temperature switch shown in figure G-13 set on "Warm wash, Cold rinse" all the switches marked with a "WC" will be closed. Take power off the machine, and remove all four wires from the switch. Test for continuity between the BU and the BR terminals; you should see good continuity. Test also between the BR-W and G-Y terminals. You should see good continuity.

Now test between the BR-W and BR terminals. There is no WC marking next to the middle switch, so the switch should be open. You should see *no* continuity with your VOM. Test the switch similarly for all settings.

2-5(e) DRIVE MOTORS, START SWITCH, AND CAPACITORS

A motor that is trying to start, but can't for whatever reason, is using one heckuva lot of electricity. So much, in fact, that if it is allowed to continue being energized in a stalled state, it will start burning wires. To prevent this, an overload switch is installed on motors to cut power to them if they don't start within a certain amount of time.

If the motor is trying to start, but can't, you will hear certain things. First will be a click, followed immediately by a buzzing sound. Then, after about 5 to 20 seconds of buzzing, another click and the buzzing will stop. The sounds will keep repeating every minute or two. In some extreme cases, you may even smell burning.

If you hear the motor doing this, but it won't start, disconnect power and take all the load off it. For example, disconnect the drive belt, pump drive system, etc.

Try to start the motor again. If it still won't start, the motor or starting capacitor is bad. If you have an ammeter, the stalled motor will be drawing 10 to 20 amps or more.

If the motor DOES start with the load removed, the pump or transmission may be locked up; See section 2-3 and 2-4(a).

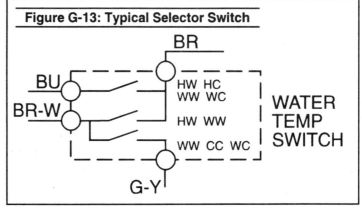

Figure G-13: Typical Selector Switch

CAPACITOR

Not all machines have external motor starting capacitors.

On machines that do, most external capacitors are mounted piggyback on the motor. (Figure G-14) A few machines have their capacitors mounted separately inside the cabinet, and a few have them mounted in other places, like behind the control console. See the chapter about *your* machine for details.

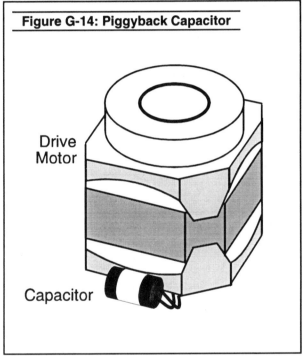

Figure G-14: Piggyback Capacitor

Drive Motor

Capacitor

If your machine has an external capacitor, unplug the machine and DISCHARGE THE CAPACITOR. BE CAREFUL; IT CAN GIVE YOU A NASTY SHOCK, *EVEN IF THE WASHER IS NOT PLUGGED IN!* You can discharge it by shorting the two terminals on your capacitor with your screwdriver. Be careful not to touch the metal part of your screwdriver with your hands while you do this.

After discharging the capacitor, disconnect its leads and test it. Set your VOM on Rx1 and touch the two test probes to the two capacitor terminals. Initially, the meter should bounce towards the right of the scale (good continuity), then slowly move back to the left side a bit as the capacitor builds resistance. Reverse the two probes on the terminals. The meter reading should act the same way. If you do not get these readings, replace the capacitor.

STARTING SWITCH

Only GE-built machines have an external, replaceable current-relay starting switch. See the GE chapter for testing.

Most other machines have a *centrifugal* starting switch mounted piggyback on the motor. Testing the switch is most easily accomplished by replacing it.

Remember that starting switches are electrical parts, which are generally not returnable. If you test the switch by replacing it, and the problem turns out to be the motor itself, you will probably not be able to return the starting switch for a refund. But they're generally pretty cheap, and if it IS the problem, you just saved yourself the best part of a hundred bucks for a new motor.

MOTOR

If your motor is stalled (buzzing and/or tripping out on the overload switch) and the capacitor and starting switch test O.K., the motor is bad. Replace it.

2-6 LEAKS

Although there are a few leaks common to all brands, most brands have leaks that are peculiar to their design. GE, Whirlpool, Maytag, and others all have common and well-known leak areas. After reading this section, see the chapter about specific brands for details.

A common "leak" zone is not a leak at all; the wall drain backs up and overflows onto the floor. This is commonly misdiagnosed as a leak. It can be difficult to diagnose; the problem may be intermittent. Depending on how badly the drain is clogged, there may be a little water or a lot, or it may only overflow every second or third load. While diagnosing a leak, do not be too quick to write this diagnosis off.

If you suspect that your drain is backing up, but you can't quite ever be there at the right time to *observe* the overflow, try this: wrap some toilet paper around the drain hose just above the wall drain pipe. If it backs up, the paper will get wet. Even if you're not there when it happens and the paper dries out, it will have crinkled up, and you'll know your drain's backing up.

If it isn't the drain, run the machine with a full load. Without moving the machine, get right down on the floor and look under the machine with a flashlight. Try to find the general area where water is dripping to the floor; front or back of the machine, left or right side.

Open the cabinet and look for mineral or soap deposits where there shouldn't be any. Trace the deposits in the natural direction of waterflow (against gravity or centrifugal force) back to the source of the leak. Fill the machine again and run it through a cycle or two. Be patient; use your eyes and your brains. There is no magic, easy way to detect a leak.

The *usual* places are:

WATER VALVE: The guts of the fill solenoid valve sometimes will corrode. You may see water leaking from, or rust on the top of the solenoid. (See figure G-15) Since the valves only open during a fill

cycle, this may appear as an intermittent leak. The solution is to replace the valve.

PUMP: Usually from around the pulley seal. Some washer pumps have a hole that allows water to weep out when the seal starts to go bad. The solution is to replace or rebuild the pump.

BLEACH DISPENSERS: Bleach is *VERY* hard on plastic parts. If the bleach dispenser gets old and brittle, it can crack or break off, and the flush water can leak out. But since the dispenser may only be flushed at certain times in the cycle, this will appear as an intermittent leak. The solution is to replace the dispenser, or if you don't use it any more, plug the hose and seal the cracked dispenser with RTV (silicone seal.)

HOSES: Though hose leaks are a bit less common than other leaks, any hoses with a few too many miles on them may be suspect. Replace the hose.

TUB: If the tub is rotted through, it's probably time to replace the washer. If a consistent imbalance in the basket has caused it to wear a hole in the tub (not an uncommon experience to GE washers) then you *may* be able to fix it with an epoxy patch. Ask your appliance parts dealer for an epoxy patch kit.

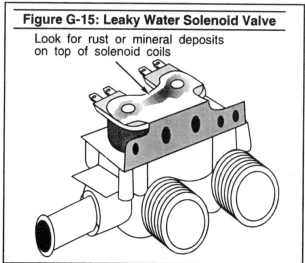

Figure G-15: Leaky Water Solenoid Valve

Look for rust or mineral deposits on top of solenoid coils

Chapter 3

WHIRLPOOL / KENMORE BELT DRIVE

The Whirlpool belt-driven design is well over thirty years old. The basic design has remained virtually unchanged in that time. Although it is extremely reliable, it does have its quirks. Fortunately, having been around for so long, the peculiarities of the design are pretty well known.

3-1 BASIC OPERATION

The design uses a single direction motor, with solenoids to engage and disengage the agitate and spin cycles and pump. (Figure W-1) The arrangement of control solenoids is peculiar to this design. It's called a "wigwag."

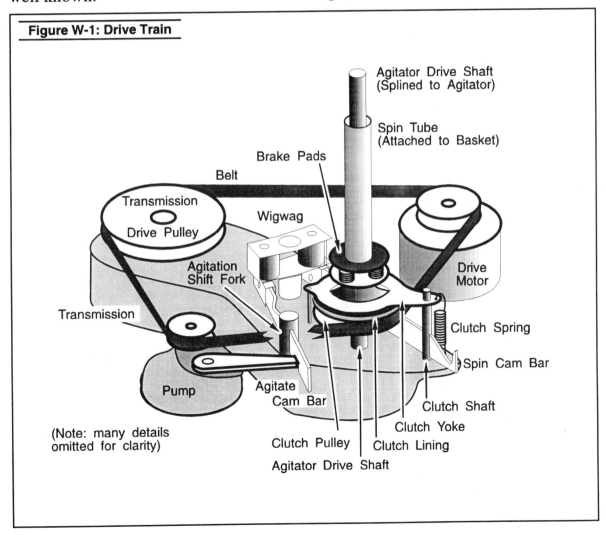

Figure W-1: Drive Train

Agitator Drive Shaft (Splined to Agitator)

Spin Tube (Attached to Basket)

Brake Pads

Belt

Transmission Drive Pulley

Wigwag

Agitation Shift Fork

Transmission

Drive Motor

Clutch Spring

Spin Cam Bar

Pump

Agitate Cam Bar

Clutch Shaft

Clutch Yoke

Clutch Pulley

Clutch Lining

Agitator Drive Shaft

(Note: many details omitted for clarity)

Whenever the motor is running, gears in the transmission keep the wigwag rotating back and forth in a motion similar to the agitator. Each solenoid's plunger is attached to a yoke with a pin through it. This pin rides in a slot in the cam bar (more about the cam bar later.)

When one of the solenoids is energized, the plunger retracts. The pin in the plunger rides in a different part of the cam bar slot than before. (Figure W-2) Since the wigwag is constantly moving back and forth, the pin will push the cam bar to a different position.

The pump turns in only one direction and has a flapper valve located within its housing. To change from recirculate to pumpout, the flapper valve changes position.

Figure W-2: Cam Bar Action

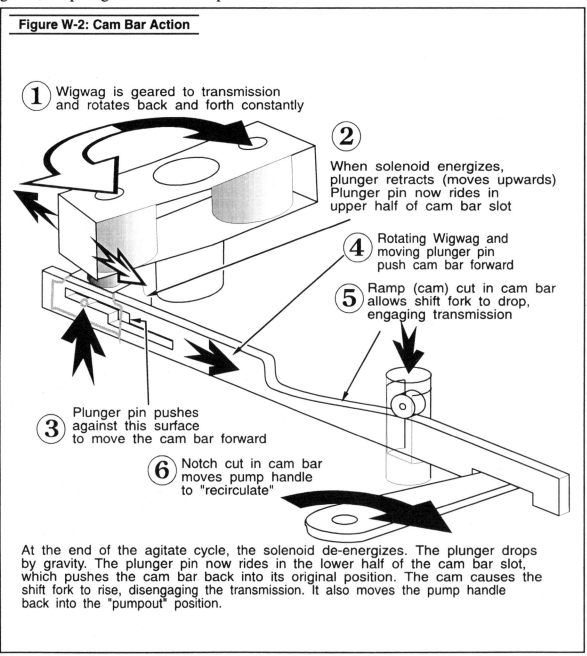

① Wigwag is geared to transmission and rotates back and forth constantly

② When solenoid energizes, plunger retracts (moves upwards) Plunger pin now rides in upper half of cam bar slot

④ Rotating Wigwag and moving plunger pin push cam bar forward

⑤ Ramp (cam) cut in cam bar allows shift fork to drop, engaging transmission

③ Plunger pin pushes against this surface to move the cam bar forward

⑥ Notch cut in cam bar moves pump handle to "recirculate"

At the end of the agitate cycle, the solenoid de-energizes. The plunger drops by gravity. The plunger pin now rides in the lower half of the cam bar slot, which pushes the cam bar back into its original position. The cam causes the shift fork to rise, disengaging the transmission. It also moves the pump handle back into the "pumpout" position.

AGITATE CYCLE

During the agitate cycle, the agitate solenoid (the solenoid on the right side of the wigwag, as you look into the back of the washer) energizes and pushes the agitate cam bar towards the front of the washer. (See Figures W-2 and W-3) The agitate cam bar does two things:

1) The ramp cut into its shape lets the agitator fork drop down towards the transmission. This engages the transmission and causes the agitator to agitate.

2) The pump lever moves, causing the pump to recirculate.

When the agitate cycle is over, power is removed from the solenoid, and the cam bar moves towards the back of the washer. This disengages the transmission and changes the pump back into the pumpout mode.

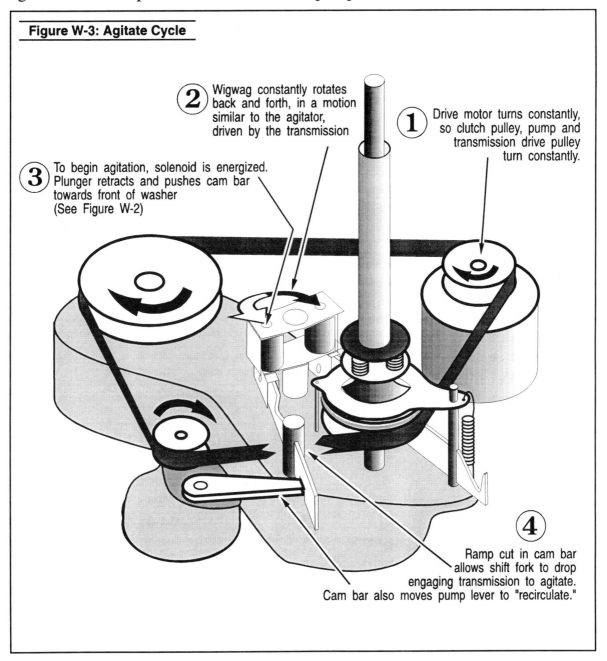

Figure W-3: Agitate Cycle

② Wigwag constantly rotates back and forth, in a motion similar to the agitator, driven by the transmission

① Drive motor turns constantly, so clutch pulley, pump and transmission drive pulley turn constantly.

③ To begin agitation, solenoid is energized. Plunger retracts and pushes cam bar towards front of washer (See Figure W-2)

④ Ramp cut in cam bar allows shift fork to drop engaging transmission to agitate. Cam bar also moves pump lever to "recirculate."

SPIN CYCLE

During the spin cycle, the spin solenoid energizes (the solenoid on the left side of the wigwag, as you look into the back of the washer.) The wigwag plunger pulls the spin cam bar towards the back of the washer. (See Figure W-4) This allows the clutch bar to drop, and the clutch spring and brake springs move the clutch yoke downward. The brake disengages and the clutch lining touches the clutch pulley. The clutch engages,

and the basket starts spinning.

When the spin cycle is over, or when the washer lid is lifted, power is removed from the solenoid. The cam bar moves towards the front of the washer, pushing the clutch bar and yoke upwards. The clutch disengages and the brake engages, bringing the basket to a rapid stop.

This whole clutch and braking assembly is known as the basket drive assembly.

Figure W-4: Spin Cycle

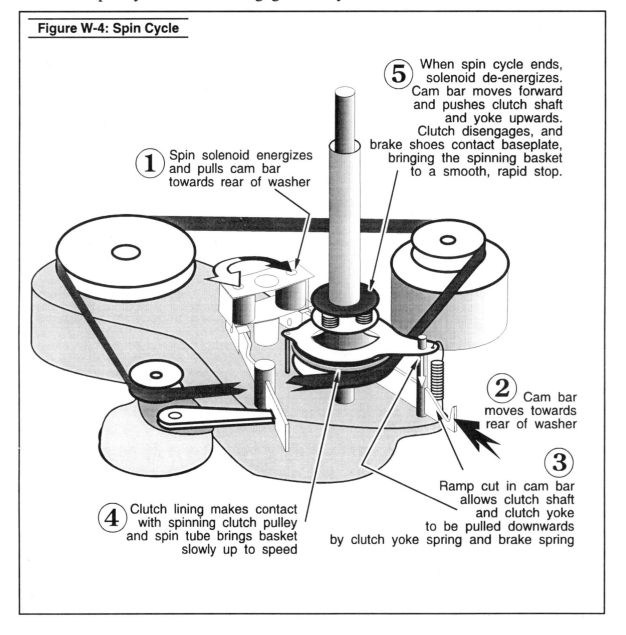

① Spin solenoid energizes and pulls cam bar towards rear of washer

⑤ When spin cycle ends, solenoid de-energizes. Cam bar moves forward and pushes clutch shaft and yoke upwards. Clutch disengages, and brake shoes contact baseplate, bringing the spinning basket to a smooth, rapid stop.

② Cam bar moves towards rear of washer

③ Ramp cut in cam bar allows clutch shaft and clutch yoke to be pulled downwards by clutch yoke spring and brake spring

④ Clutch lining makes contact with spinning clutch pulley and spin tube brings basket slowly up to speed

3-2 OPENING THE CABINET AND CONSOLE

See figure W-5 for details about opening the cabinet and console.

In raising the lid of the washer, it is better to use a putty knife. You can use a thin-bladed screwdriver, but you might chip or scratch the paint.

A wiring diagram is usually pasted to the back of the machine.

3-3 DIAGNOSIS

Diagnosis begins by checking to see exactly which cycles the washer is missing or malfunctioning in. For example, if the washer won't drain or spin, check also to see if it will agitate before you empty the tub. In this type of washer, you can pretty well narrow down the cause just by knowing the exact symptoms.

Here are the most common complaints:

DIAGNOSIS 1: THE WASHER AGITATES BUT WON'T DRAIN OR SPIN.

In this design, the water level interlocks the spin cycle. The washer will only spin if the water is pumped almost all the way out. If the pump is not pumping out water, the washer will not begin to spin. Check for a kinked drain hose. Also check the pump as described in Section 3-10. Often there will be a strong burning smell along with this problem. This is almost always a locked pump; the burning smell comes from the stopped rubber belt riding on the turning motor pulley.

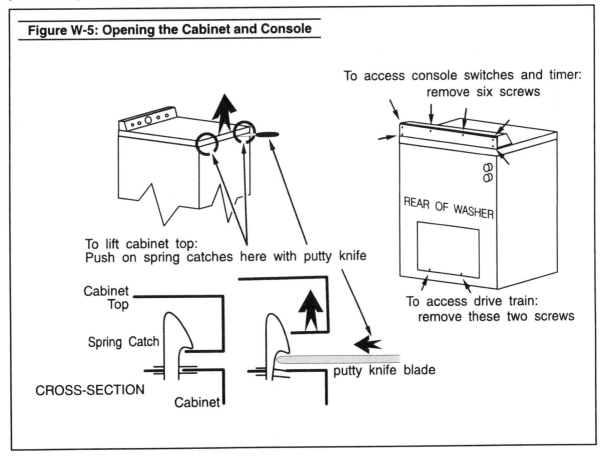

Figure W-5: Opening the Cabinet and Console

To access console switches and timer:
remove six screws

REAR OF WASHER

To access drive train:
remove these two screws

To lift cabinet top:
Push on spring catches here with putty knife

Cabinet Top

Spring Catch

CROSS-SECTION

Cabinet

putty knife blade

DIAGNOSIS 2: THE WASHER AGITATES AND DRAINS BUT WON'T SPIN. (Clothes are dripping wet at end of cycle.)

Something is interrupting either the electrical spin circuit or the mechanical spin mechanism.

The basket will not start spinning if the lid is up. A bad lid switch will have the same effect. Close the lid; if the basket still does not spin, check the lid switch for continuity. Also check to see that the switch striker is not broken off.

If this doesn't solve the problem, test for power at the left (spin) wigwag solenoid when in the spin cycle. The easiest way to do this is to unplug the washer and switch the red and yellow wigwag leads as shown in figure W-6. Plug the washer in and set it in the SPIN cycle. If it AGITATES, then you are getting power to the solenoid. Either the wigwag solenoid itself is bad, or the clutch is worn out.

Put the wires back on the correct terminals and watch the spin cam bar as you start the washer in "spin." If the spin cam bar does not move, the wigwag is bad; replace it as described in section 3-11. Check also for a broken pin in the plunger. If the spin cam bar DOES move, the clutch is worn out; see section 3-15.

If switching the wires does NOT cause the washer to agitate, then put the two leads back on the correct terminals and check the following:

The water level is sensed by the water level switch. If the switch is bad, the washer will not spin. Test the switch as described in sections 3-4 and 2-5(b).

Often one of the wigwag wires will break, usually very near the wigwag itself. Furthermore, the break may be internal; you will see no damage on the outside of the wire. Test the wires for continuity and repair if bad.

The timer contacts may be bad. Test for continuity through the spin solenoid circuit of the timer as described in section 2-5(c). If there is no continuity, replace the timer as described in section 3-5.

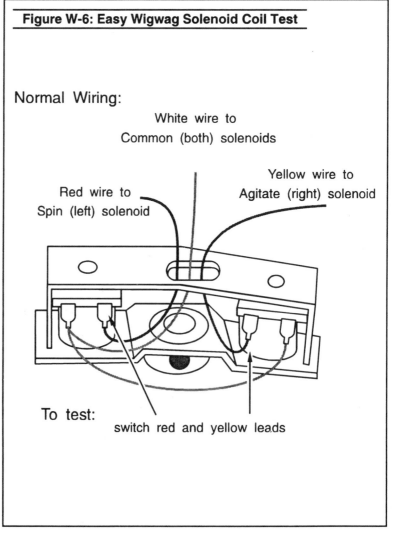

Figure W-6: Easy Wigwag Solenoid Coil Test

Normal Wiring:

White wire to
Common (both) solenoids

Red wire to
Spin (left) solenoid

Yellow wire to
Agitate (right) solenoid

To test: switch red and yellow leads

DIAGNOSIS 3: THE WASHER FILLS BUT WON'T AGITATE, DRAIN OR SPIN.

The belt is probably broken; replace as described in section 3-13.

If the motor hums, but does not turn, Check as described in section 2-5(e). If the motor turns with no load, check the drive pulley and pump pulley to see which is locked. If the motor doesn't start with no load, replace it as described in section 3-12.

If you don't even hear the motor hum, the motor, motor starting switch or capacitor may be bad; see section 3-12. Also check the motor circuits of the timer as described in section 2-5(c). Also check for a locked transmission as described in section 2-4(c). If the transmission is locked, see section 3-14.

DIAGNOSIS 4: THE WASHER WON'T AGITATE, BUT DOES FILL, DRAIN AND SPIN.

When you set the timer at the beginning of a wash cycle, the fill solenoid valve opens first. When the water level switch senses the correct water level, the solenoid valve closes, the motor starts, and the agitation (right) wigwag solenoid energizes.

Usually this problem is a burnt out agitation solenoid, but there are other possibilities.

To test the agitation solenoid, switch the wigwag leads as shown in Figure W-6. Make sure the tub is full and start the washer somewhere in the AGITATE cycle. If the basket SPINS, then you're getting power to the wigwag. Either the agitate wigwag coil is burnt or the plunger or pin is broken.

Another possibility is that the agitator spline is stripped, as described in section

3-13. If the washer agitates very weakly, i.e. you can stop the agitator with your hands, this is a very strong possibility.

The last possibility is that the transmission is broken internally. See section 3-14.

NOTE: The lid switch is NOT interlocked with the agitate cycle in these machines; they WILL agitate with the lid up.

DIAGNOSIS 5: THE WASHER DOES ABSOLUTELY NOTHING; NO FILL, AGITATE, DRAIN OR SPIN.

Check for power to the machine.

Check the main power circuit through the timer; it may have bad contacts. See section 2-5(c).

Check the imbalance switch. (Kenmore models ONLY) See section 3-6.

DIAGNOSIS 6: THE WASHER IS VERY NOISY IN SPIN OR WHEN BRAKING.

The clutch or brake linings are probably badly worn. If so, replacing the basket drive will solve your noise problem. See section 3-15.

If the centerpost (spin tube) bearings are worn, replacing the basket drive will not solve your noise problem. You will need to call a *qualified* service technician to replace the bearings, or simply junk the washer. (I stress the word *qualified*, because it is a specialized job that many technicians will not tackle.)

The way to tell the difference is to listen to the noise the machine is making. If the machine is making a squealing or groaning noise, the problem is more likely to be the basket drive. If it is more like a rattling sound, the centerpost bearings are probably worn out.

A secondary check is to look at the clutch lining. On late models, there are three little pads riveted to the clutch plate. (Figure W-7) Older models had a full disc lining, rather than the three little pads. The lining touches the clutch pulley directly when the clutch is engaged. If it gets worn too badly, the rivets will screech against the clutch pulley. Take a look at the pads or lining. If it looks too thin, it's probably worn out. Also inspect the clutch surface on top of the pulley for any scoring or gouging. If there is any, your clutch is worn out. Replace the basket drive assembly as described in section 3-15.

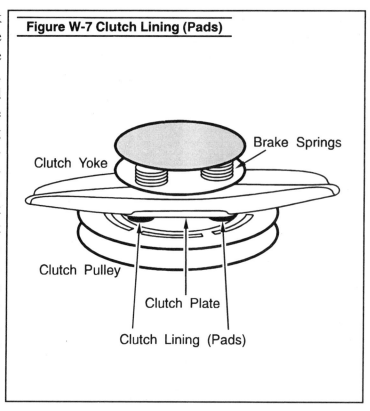

Figure W-7 Clutch Lining (Pads)

Brake Springs

Clutch Yoke

Clutch Pulley

Clutch Plate

Clutch Lining (Pads)

DIAGNOSIS 7: THE WASHER LEAKS.

See section 2-6 on leaks and backed up drains.

On these machines, leaks usually come from the pump (section 3-10) or the air dome or other tub fitting (section 3-9.) Sometimes, there will be a leak in the fill hose, or in a bleach or softener dispenser.

DIAGNOSIS 8: EXCESSIVE VIBRATION WHEN SPINNING

If redistributing the clothes doesn't seem to help, see Section 3-7 on replacing the snubber and cleaning the snubber pad.

DIAGNOSIS 9: INTERMITTENT SYMPTOMS.

Usually, with intermittent problems, you simply must know the system and just look at things until you see something malfunctioning.

Some intermittent problems may be traceable to electrical problems, such as a loose terminal or worn wire. However, most intermittent problems with these machines come from mechanical causes.

For example, if the belt is loose, the machine may not spin sometimes, may not pump out at other times, and still other times it may not agitate. The solution is obviously to tighten the belt (or replace it if it is badly worn.)

Another aggravating and difficult to diagnose symptom is caused by worn cam bars. The washer may appear to slip in and out of the spin cycle at very short intervals. Or it may start spinning and suddenly stop, then restart a minute later.

If the washer tries to spin and agitate at the same time, it usually means that the spin plunger is bent, or the spin cam bar is badly worn.

There is also a very stiff leaf spring that holds the cam bars down in place (Figure W-8.) The bolt that holds this leaf spring in place has been known to back out, or the spring can break, causing all sorts of strange symptoms. The bolt can be replaced without removing the transmission, but it's a real bear of a job.

3-4 WATER LEVEL SWITCH

The water level switch is located in the control panel on top of the cabinet. For access to the switch, see section 3-2. Test the switch as described in section 2-5(b), using figure W-9. If the water level switch is bad, replace it.

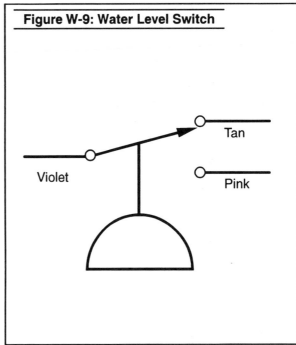

Figure W-9: Water Level Switch

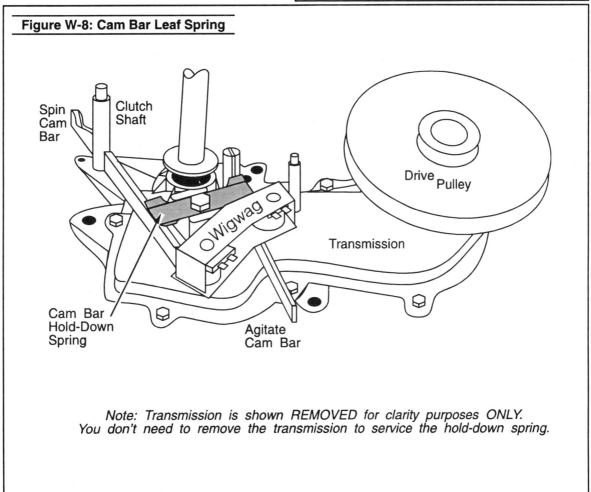

Figure W-8: Cam Bar Leaf Spring

Note: Transmission is shown REMOVED for clarity purposes ONLY.
You don't need to remove the transmission to service the hold-down spring.

3-5 TIMER

Test the timer as described in section 2-5(c).

Two types of timers were used: standard frame and quick-disconnect. (See Figure W-10)

To replace a defective timer, first unplug the washer. Pull the knob out, hold the timer dial and turn the timer knob to the left to unscrew it. (Figure W-10)

The standard frame timer has a locknut that holds the timer dial on and six splines that keep it in place on the timer shaft. When re-installing the dial, you must get it in the right part of the cycle. It can only go on the shaft in six different ways. If you've replaced the timer, you just have play with the dial until you get on the right way.

The quick-disconnect has a D-shaped shaft that the timer dial just slips onto.

Remove the locknut, if necessary, and remove the timer dial. Remove the two timer mounting screws from the front of the console. If you have a standard frame timer, mark the timer wires before removing them, so you can get them on the correct terminals of the new timer. Better yet, if you can remove the wires from the old timer and put them directly on the new timer, one by one, it can be faster and easier.

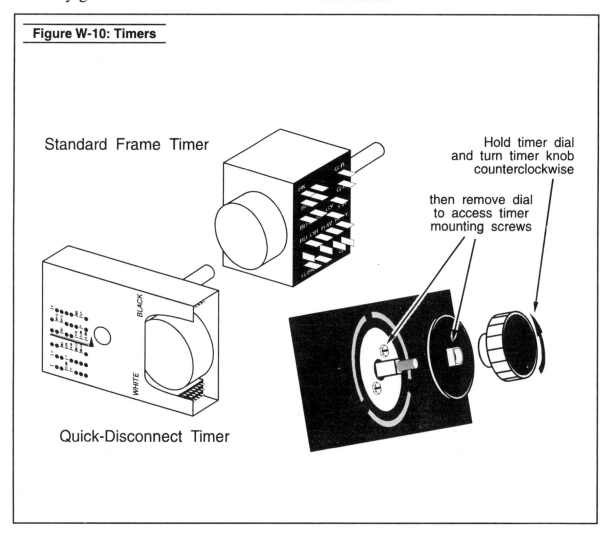

Figure W-10: Timers

Standard Frame Timer

Quick-Disconnect Timer

Hold timer dial and turn timer knob counterclockwise

then remove dial to access timer mounting screws

Figure W-11: Imbalance Switch

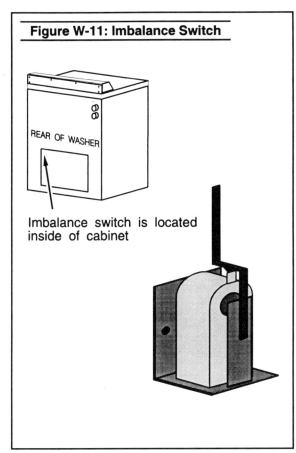

REAR OF WASHER

Imbalance switch is located inside of cabinet

3-6 IMBALANCE SWITCH (Kenmore only)

In SOME Kenmore models only, there is an imbalance switch mounted inside the cabinet (on the left side, as you look at it from the back.)(Figure W-11.) If the load is not balanced, the base plate (to which the tub is attached) will move around until it contacts the imbalance switch. The motor will cut off and a buzzer will sound. The buzzer is built into the imbalance switch.

Usually, when they go bad, the washer will intermittently cut out for no apparent reason. You may also see a bright flash; this is the switch arcing. Sometimes, the switch may burn out altogether and it will seem as if the machine isn't getting any power at all. This switch is easy to replace; just remember to unplug the machine first.

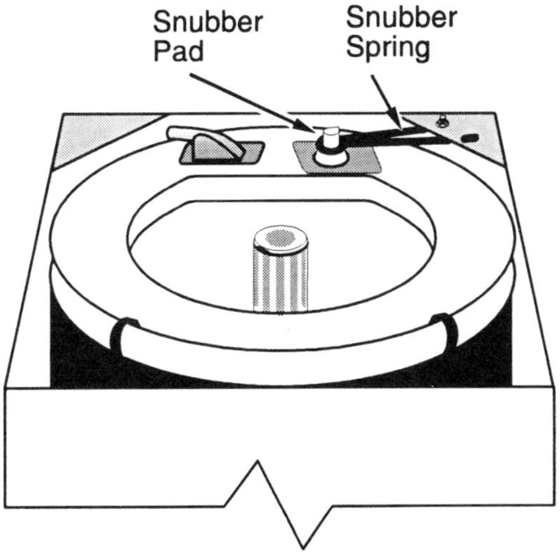

3-7 SNUBBER AND SNUBBER PAD

If the washer vibrates too badly, and redistributing the clothes doesn't seem to help, it could be that the snubber spring is broken, or that the snubber block or pad is choked up with soap.

Unplug the washer and raise the lid.

The snubber is in the right rear corner of the washer. (Figure W-12) Lift the spring (there's a lot of tension on it) to remove the snubber block. Be careful not to catch your fingers under the spring!

To remove the spring, remove the single nut and bolt that hold it in place, and twist it out of its mounts.

Clean the snubber pad by wiping it with a wet towel or sponge.

Roughen the face of the snubber block a little with sandpaper, or simply take it outside and rub it on the sidewalk or a brick surface.

Figure W-12: Snubber and Snubber Spring

Snubber Pad   Snubber Spring

3-8 AGITATOR REPLACEMENT

Your agitator is splined to the transmission driveshaft, and secured with a stud. Access to the stud is in one of two ways. (Figure W-13) Some have a removable plastic cap on top; you simply pry it off with a screwdriver, and you will see the stud with a nut on it. In others, a one-piece threaded cap is screwed directly to the stud itself. To remove the threaded cap or nut, hold the agitator (this will keep the driveshaft from turning) and unscrew.

But what if the agitator splines are stripped? You can hold the agitator all you want, and the shaft will keep turning with the nut or the threaded cap.

Here's a good confirmation of a stripped spline. Put the timer in an agitate cycle. Let the washer fill and begin to agitate. If you can hold the agitator still, and the nut or cap is reciprocating back and forth, the spline is probably stripped.

Here's a little trick to get the nut or cap off when you can't hold the shaft still; let the *machinery* hold it still *for you.*

If you have a nut & stud, hit the nut with a little WD-40 and put a ratchet on it. Make sure the ratchet is set for the proper direction; to *remove* the nut. Hold the rachet and start your washer in the agitation cycle. The nut will back off with each sweep of the agitator shaft.

If you have a threaded cap, you can do the same thing by hand. Simply start the machine in the agitate cycle and turn the cap counterclockwise.

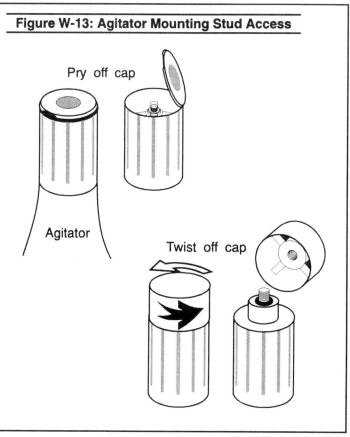

Figure W-13: Agitator Mounting Stud Access

Pry off cap

Agitator

Twist off cap

3-9 BASKET REMOVAL AND TUB FITTINGS

To replace any leaking tub fittings, you must remove the basket.

Unplug the washer and raise the cabinet top as described in section 3-2.

Remove the agitator as described in section 3-8.

Remove the snubber spring as described in section 3-7.

Remove the water inlet fitting from the tub ring. (Figure W-14)

Carefully note the sizes and positions of the tub ring clips as you remove them.(Figure W-14.

Remove the spanner nut. (Figure W-15) A special tool is available from your appliance parts dealer. The tool is a very common item and thus is pretty cheap.

Lift the basket straight up and out.

Figure W-14: Tub Ring Area

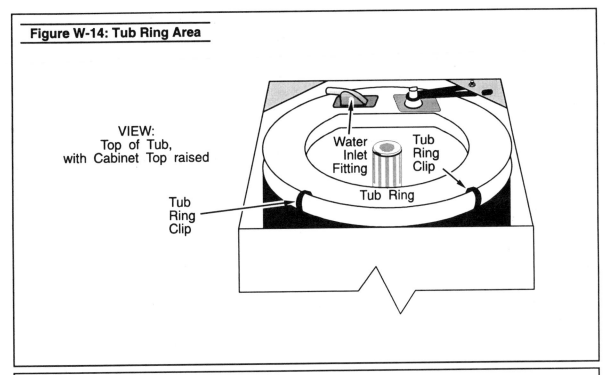

VIEW:
Top of Tub,
with Cabinet Top raised

Water Inlet Fitting

Tub Ring Clip

Tub Ring

Tub Ring Clip

Figure W-15: Spanner Nut

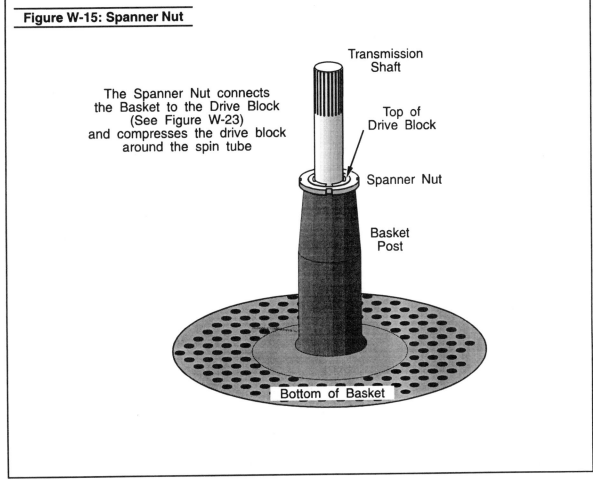

The Spanner Nut connects
the Basket to the Drive Block
(See Figure W-23)
and compresses the drive block
around the spin tube

Transmission Shaft

Top of Drive Block

Spanner Nut

Basket Post

Bottom of Basket

INSTALLATION is basically the opposite of removal.

Most of the tub fittings have rubber seals and locking nuts or rings. Simply twist the ring counterclockwise to remove.

The air dome is the fitting that attaches the water pressure switch hose to the tub. It is a common source of leaks. To remove the dome, remove the hose from it and turn it 90 degrees to unlock it from the seal.

3-10 PUMPS

In this design, the basket will not start spinning until almost all the water is pumped out of the tub.

Whirlpool washers were equipped, at various times, with three different pumps. (Figure W-16) In the parts houses, they are commonly known as two-hose, three-hose, and four-hose pumps, for obvious reasons. Whirlpool pumps cannot be rebuilt; they must be replaced. Fortunately, they're very common items, so they are pretty cheap.

REMOVAL

Drain the tub. Remove the back panel of the washer. Loosen the motor mounting bolts and remove tension from the belt.

Lean the washer back against the wall, following the safety tips in section 1-5. Put a bucket underneath the pump and remove the hoses. Pull out the two mounting bolts and remove the pump. Rocking the pump away from the drive belt will help disengage the belt, and also the pump lever from the cam bar. DO NOT MOVE THE PUMP LEVER YET.

Check the belt for wear as described in section 2-4(a), especially for burned or glazed spots where it rode over the locked pump pulley or motor drive pulley. Replace the belt if it is worn, following the instructions in section 3-13.

INSTALLATION

Set the pump lever in the same position as the pump that came out. Rock the pump in place, the same way as you pulled the old one out. Make sure the pump lever goes into the slot in the agitate cam bar, and install the mounting bolts. Tension the belt as described in section 3-13.

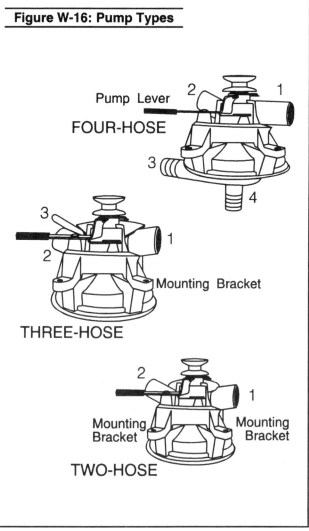

Figure W-16: Pump Types

3-11 WIGWAG AND CAM BARS

The wigwag is located inside the back panel of the machine. Replacement is fairly easy. First, take all power off the machine. Note which color wires go to which wigwag terminals and remove the wires. Loosen the wigwag setscrew and pull the wigwag straight off the shaft. Replace the wigwag directly, taking care to get the right wires on the right terminals. Also make sure that the plungers fit loosely in the wigwag so that they can move freely. Replace the setscrew, making sure it goes in the hole on the wigwag drive shaft, and tighten securely.

Normally, you will not need to replace the plungers, even when you replace the wigwag. If you see that one is bent or the pin is badly worn, replace the plunger.

The plungers can be quite difficult to replace. The pins that connect them to the cam bars are hardened and thus difficult to cut through.

The first step is to remove power from the machine and cut through the pin. Use a hacksaw blade, diagonals or bolt cutters. Clearance is tight. Sometimes it's easier to hacksaw through the body of the yoke than to cut the pin.

Once you've cut through the pin, remove the wigwag as described above and replace the plunger, using the instructions that come with the new plunger. Make sure you install the plastic insert. It keeps the machine quieter.

To replace the spin cam bar, you must drop the transmission slightly as described in section 3-13. To replace the agitate cam bar, you must remove the transmission as described in section 3-14.

3-12 DRIVE MOTOR

Single speed, two-speed and three-speed motors were used at different times in these washers. The different motors were, at times, produced by different manufacturers. When you're replacing a motor, capacitor or motor starting switch, you'll need either numbers off the motor or switch you're replacing, or a model number for the washer, to make sure you get the right parts.

NOTE: On two-and three-speed machines (Those that have a "permanent press" setting on the timer dial) a timer failure was usually the cause of a motor failure. If you replace the motor in one of these machines, you must replace the timer, too.

TESTING

Some of these machines have external capacitors mounted either piggyback on the motor or just inside the left side of the cabinet (as you look at the back of the washer.) If yours does, DISCHARGE IT and test it as described in section 2-5(e) before doing any work on the motor.

Now test the start switch as described in section 2-5(e).

If your capacitor and motor starting switch test O.K., replace the drive motor. It is held in place by two mounting nuts.

3-13 DRIVE BELT

Open the back of the machine and inspect the belt as described in section 2-4(a).

If the belt is broken, make sure you check the pump and transmission pulleys to see if they are locked. This may be the cause of the belt breaking.

REPLACING THE BELT

Unfortunately, the belt is not easy to replace on this machine. To get the belt past the clutch shaft, you actually have to drop the transmission out slightly, and sometimes the transmission needs to be realigned afterwards. Here are the steps:

1) Prepare the machine: Unplug it, siphon out any water, and lay it down on its front side using the safety instructions in section 1-5(4). Remove the back panel.

2) Remove the clutch yoke spring, (Figure W-17)

3) Remove the braces and pump mounting bolts (Figure W-18)

4) Remove the lower left transmission mounting bolt. That is the mounting bolt next to the clutch shaft. Make sure you save the spacer that falls out.

Figure W-17: Clutch Yoke Spring

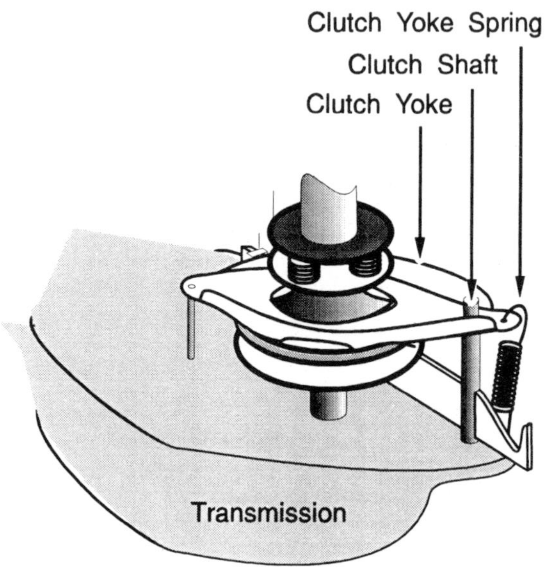

Figure W-18: Transmission Braces and Pump Mounting Bolts

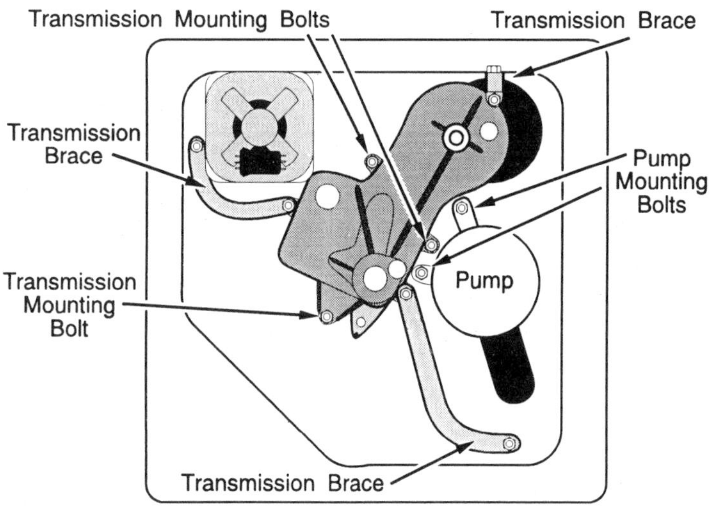

5) You must bottom out the clutch shaft. Hold the wigwag's "spin" plunger up and tap the spin cam bar towards the back of the machine. The clutch shaft will drop down towards the bottom of the machine. (Figure W-19)

6) Loosen the two other transmission mounting bolts about 7 full turns. Then pull the transmission straight out until it stops against the bolts.

7) Remove the belt. If you have trouble getting it over the clutch shaft, back out the transmission mounting bolts another turn or two.

Figure W-19: Bottoming the Clutch Shaft

Tap Cam Bar Back
So That The Clutch Shaft Drops Down
As Far As It Will Go

INSTALLING THE BELT

Installation is basically the opposite of removal, except for the following:

1) Look at the transmission shaft, right where it comes out of the transmission and goes up into the basket drive. On most models, you will see a plastic "T"-bearing. (Figure W-20) This "T"-bearing is connected to the shaft by a ball; the ball fits in a hole in the shaft and a slot in the "T"-bearing. Make sure the ball is in the hole in the transmission shaft, and that the slot in the "T"-bearing fits down over the ball, before you tighten the transmission mounting bolts.

NOTE: Some models used a "C"-clip rather than a ball to hold the "T"-bearing in place. If you have one of these, ignore this step.

Figure W-20: "T"-Bearing

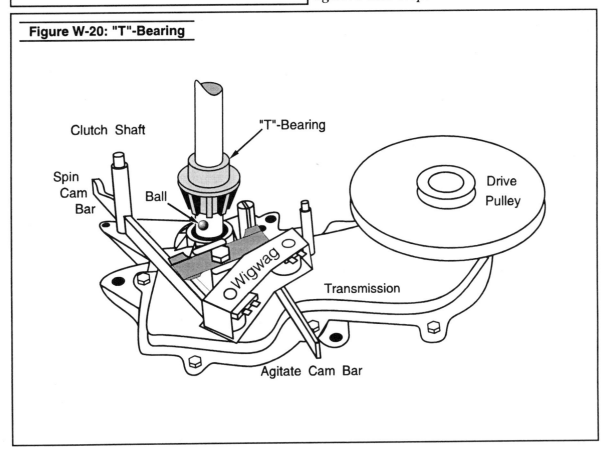

Clutch Shaft

Spin
Cam
Bar

Ball

"T"-Bearing

Wigwag

Drive
Pulley

Transmission

Agitate Cam Bar

2) The top of the clutch shaft has either two washers or a hex nut on it. Make sure these are replaced before you bolt the transmission back into place.

3) Make sure you replace the spacer before installing the lower left mounting bolt.

4) To set the correct tension on the belt, loosen the motor mounts and move the motor by hand. DO NOT use a lever or pry bar to set tension. The belt should deflect about 1/2" by hand, with easy pressure. (6 lbs is the official number, though there's no real practical way to measure it)

If the belt has never been adjusted before replacement, the new belt will probably not require adjusting. Make sure that the belt rides over all four pulleys: the pump pulley, the transmission drive pulley, the motor pulley and the clutch pulley.

5) You *may* get the machine all back together and find that the spin cycle has problems. The machine may not spin at all, or it may spin very slowly. If so, the transmission needs to be aligned. This is a tricky procedure, so be careful:

Remove the three braces from the transmission. Back off your three transmission mounting bolts about 1/2 to 1 turn; just enough so the transmission will drift a little. The transmission should be just slightly loose, and all three bolts must be backed out the same amount.

Set your washer upright and level. Make sure there is no water or clothes in the basket, and START THE WASHER IN THE SPIN CYCLE. Let it get up to speed, then stop the washer. Unplug it.

Without moving the washer, tighten the three transmission mounting bolts beneath it as evenly as possible. Test the machine to see that it still spins properly. If not, repeat the procedure. When you have it spinning properly, replace the three braces.

3-14 TRANSMISSION

If the transmission locks up, you will need to replace it; don't try to rebuild it yourself. They are pretty standard items; most appliance parts dealers carry rebuilt Whirlpool transmissions in stock. Make sure you bring the old transmission with you; they will need to match shaft lengths and there will probably be an exchange or a core charge.

To replace the transmission, follow the same instructions as in section 3-13, with the following additional steps:

1) Remove the agitator, as described in section 3-8.

2) Mark and remove the wigwag wires.

3) Remove the mounting bolts all the way.

4) Snap the yoke retainer out of the plastic clip on the clutch yoke (NOTE: some models used a spring clip rather than a plastic snap arrangement.) (Figure W-21)

5) Pull the transmission straight out.

When you get the transmission out, exchange all the old parts: cam bars and spring, clutch shaft, wigwag, "T"-bearing and ball, and the transmission drive pulley. If you wish, you can replace the cam bars, T-bearing and ball as insur-

Figure W-21: Yoke Retainer

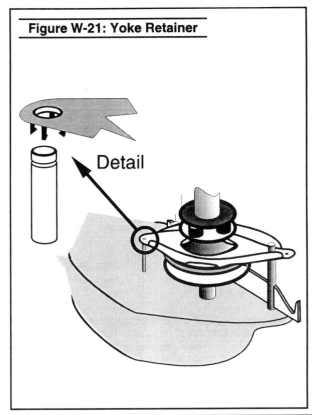

Detail

ance against future problems. Two points to remember in exchanging the parts:

1) The drive pulley is originally assembled with a drop of glue on the setscrew threads. You may need to heat the hub of the drive pulley with a torch to get the setscrew out.

2) To get the agitator cam bar out, you will need to lift the agitator shaft. The easiest way to do this is to remove the "T"-bearing ball and pry the shaft upwards with a screwdriver, as shown in Figure W-22.

Installation is basically the opposite of removal. Make sure you read "INSTALLING THE BELT" in section 3-13.

Figure W-22: Removing the Agitator Cam Bar

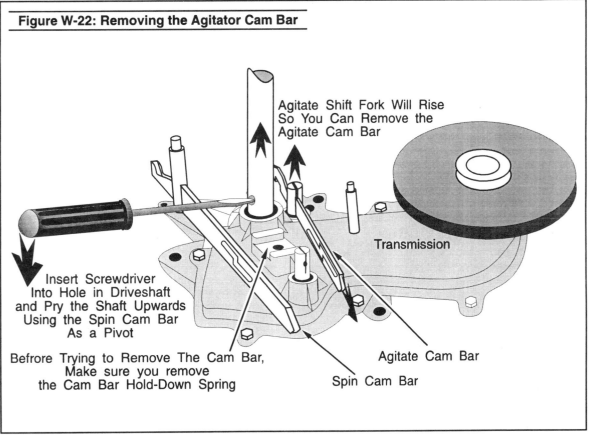

Agitate Shift Fork Will Rise So You Can Remove the Agitate Cam Bar

Transmission

Insert Screwdriver Into Hole in Driveshaft and Pry the Shaft Upwards Using the Spin Cam Bar As a Pivot

Befrore Trying to Remove The Cam Bar, Make sure you remove the Cam Bar Hold-Down Spring

Agitate Cam Bar

Spin Cam Bar

3-15 BASKET DRIVE

You cannot service the basket drive assembly, but you can replace it if the clutch or brake pads are worn. The basket drive assembly is not too terribly expensive.

To remove the basket drive assembly:

1) Remove the agitator as described in section 3-8.

2) Remove the basket as described in section 3-9.

3) Remove the drive block by tapping on the underside of it with a small hammer. (Figure W-23)

Note: The metal of the drive block is pretty soft, so don't hit it too hard--just tap it. Also be careful not to hit the tub, or you may chip the porcelain interior.

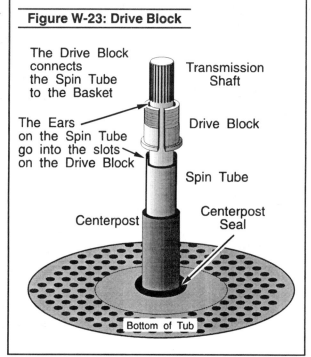

Figure W-23: Drive Block

The Drive Block connects the Spin Tube to the Basket

Transmission Shaft

The Ears on the Spin Tube go into the slots on the Drive Block

Drive Block

Spin Tube

Centerpost

Centerpost Seal

Bottom of Tub

4) Remove the transmission as described in section 3-14.

5) Pull the whole basket drive assembly straight out. Be careful not to damage the lower seal. (Figure W-24) If the lower seal pulls out with the basket drive, there is a special grease you can put in it. Ask your appliance parts dealer for some. Put the grease in the groove of the seal and put the seal back in place, groove side up.

Installation is basically the opposite of removal. However, note the following:

1) Put the basket drive in slowly so you don't damage any of the seals or bearings that it has to pass through in the centerpost.

2) Make sure that the tabs on the top of the spin tube fit in the notches in the drive block.

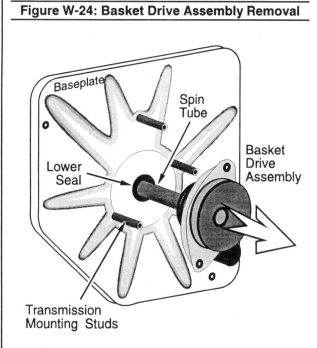

Figure W-24: Basket Drive Assembly Removal

Baseplate

Spin Tube

Basket Drive Assembly

Lower Seal

Transmission Mounting Studs

Chapter 4

WHIRLPOOL / KENMORE DIRECT DRIVE

In the early 80's, Whirlpool completely redesigned their standard washing machine model. The result is the "Design 2000" series, known in the parts houses as "Whirlpool direct drive" models.

The most profound feature of the design is that it does away with all drive belts. The motor is coupled directly to the transmission and pump. Other major changes include a new pedestal tub mounting system, a plastic tub with integral tub fittings, a liquid-ring basket balancing mechanism, and a mechanically direct-reversing transmission. Also, most of the component parts of the washer are held in place by spring clips or just a few screws, making them easy to replace.

They seem to be very good designs. The early ones had a transmission design flaw involving plastic gearing, but the flaw was designed out of the later models. About the only problems we see commonly now are leaky pumps, easily diagnosed and fixed. Still, in case you run across an early model with a bad tranny, we have included transmission replacement in this chapter.

4-1 BASIC SYSTEM (Figure DD-1)

This design uses a direct-reversing motor. In various models, single-speed, two-speed and three-speed motors were used.

A pump is mounted directly on the motor by spring clips. The pump moves water only during the spin cycle; during agitate, it is turning but it does not circulate water.

The motor is coupled directly to the transmission through a plastic and rubber flexible coupling.

Both the pump and transmission couplings will break away in the event of a transmission lockup, preventing damage to the motor.

A clutch drum and shoes (mounted atop the transmission) allow the basket to come up to speed slowly during the spin cycle. The clutch drum rotates and is driven by gears inside the transmission. Similarly, a set of brake shoes (attached to the spin tube) contact a drum (attached to the bottom of the mounting pedestal) to provide a basket braking action to the tub whenever the washer is NOT in the spin cycle.

Changing between the agitate and spin cycles is accomplished mechanically within the transmission when the motor reverses.

4-2 OPENING THE CABINET AND CONSOLE

To service the timer or other electrical controls, remove the two screws from the base of the control console as shown in Figure DD-2.

In order to service just about anything else in the washer, you must remove the whole cabinet as shown in Figure DD-2. If you need more space when performing a particular operation, you can twist the tab in the bottom center of the back

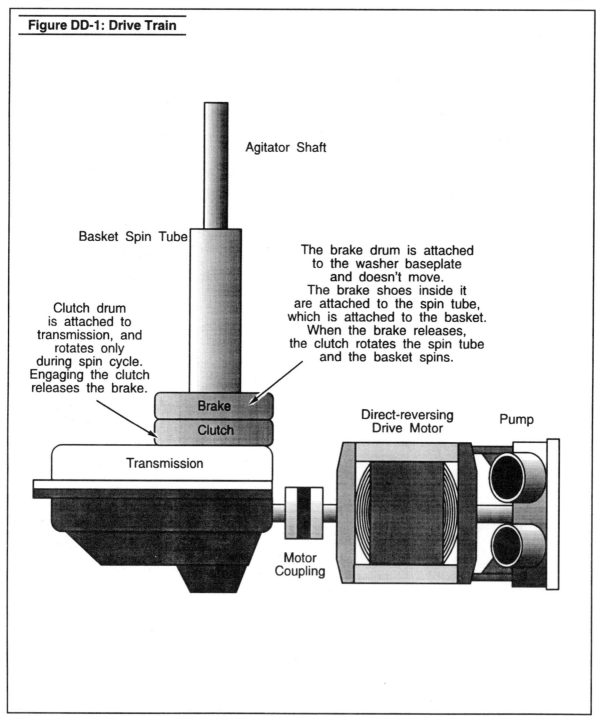

Figure DD-1: Drive Train

Agitator Shaft

Basket Spin Tube

The brake drum is attached to the washer baseplate and doesn't move. The brake shoes inside it are attached to the spin tube, which is attached to the basket. When the brake releases, the clutch rotates the spin tube and the basket spins.

Clutch drum is attached to transmission, and rotates only during spin cycle. Engaging the clutch releases the brake.

Brake

Clutch

Transmission

Direct-reversing Drive Motor

Pump

Motor Coupling

of the cabinet. This will allow the back panel to drop away from the washer a little.

To change the transmission, you will need to remove the bottom panel as shown in Figure DD-2.

It *is* possible to service the pump and motor by removing the bottom panel, but I do not recommend it. Space is tight and it can be very difficult. The pump is especially difficult; getting the hose clamps on and off can be a real son-of-a-gun. Better to just remove the cabinet.

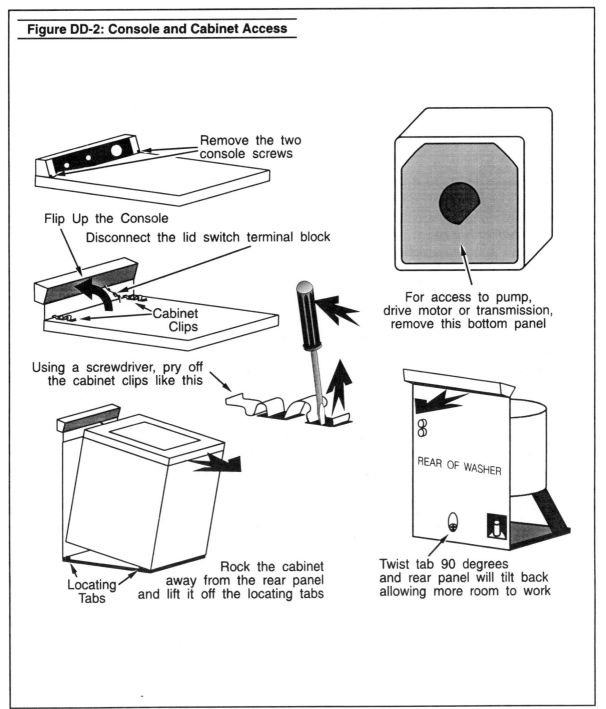

Figure DD-2: Console and Cabinet Access

Remove the two console screws

Flip Up the Console
Disconnect the lid switch terminal block

Cabinet Clips

Using a screwdriver, pry off the cabinet clips like this

For access to pump, drive motor or transmission, remove this bottom panel

REAR OF WASHER

Locating Tabs

Rock the cabinet away from the rear panel and lift it off the locating tabs

Twist tab 90 degrees and rear panel will tilt back allowing more room to work

4-3 DIAGNOSIS

After removing the cabinet, the machine can be started for testing by jumpering the lid switch leads. As always, when operating the machine without the cabinet, be careful not to touch any live electrical or moving parts.

NOISY OPERATION

A grinding noise during the agitate or spin cycle *may* mean that the motor coupling is damaged, but usually it is coming from the transmission. If so, replace the transmission. (Sections 4-8 & 4-9).

LEAKS

Any leaks are likely to be coming from one of three places:

1) The pump. See section 4-4.

2) Early models had a small problem with the drain hose nipple (where the drain hose attaches to the back of the washer.) It used a spring-type hose clamp, which was prone to coming off. (Figure DD-3) Remove the clamp and replace it with a regular stainless steel worm-type clamp.

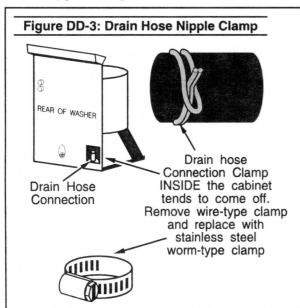

Figure DD-3: Drain Hose Nipple Clamp

REAR OF WASHER

Drain Hose Connection

Drain hose Connection Clamp INSIDE the cabinet tends to come off. Remove wire-type clamp and replace with stainless steel worm-type clamp

3) The centerpost seal can leak. Look for water coming from underneath the center of the tub. To replace, see section 4-7.

NOT PUMPING

If the motor is turning, but the tub will not drain, replace the pump as described in section 4-4. Often the pump has failed because the impeller has disintegrated, so make sure that you clear the hoses (especially the drain hose) when changing the pump.

If the motor is not turning, see section 4-8.

NOT AGITATING AND/OR SPINNING

Check the usual things, i.e. main power, timer, switches, etc. as described in sections 2-5(a) thru (e). There is an unusual timer problem that sometimes pops up in these machines; see section 2-5(c).

If spin is O.K. but the washer is not agitating, check for a stripped agitator spline as described in section 4-5.

If the motor is not turning, see section 4-8.

If the motor is turning, remove the motor as described in section 4-8 and check the transmission coupling. If it is badly damaged or destroyed, the transmission has locked up. See section 4-9.

If the motor is turning, and the transmission coupling looks okay, the transmission may be broken internally, or the clutch or brake may be malfunctioning. Remove the transmission as described in section 4-9 and check both the springs and linings on the clutch and brake. If the springs are broken or the linings are worn, replace as described in section 4-10. Usually there will be a squealing noise associated with worn clutch or brake shoes.

If the clutch and brake are O.K., try turning the transmission input shaft by hand. Turn in both directions and see if the output shaft and clutch drum are doing anything. If not, something has broken inside the transmission. Replace it.

TUB WON'T BALANCE (Even after you redistribute the clothes)

See section 4-6. Also look to see if any of the suspension springs mentioned in section 4-7 are broken.

4-4 PUMP

To get to the pump, remove the cabinet as described in section 4-2.

Have a bucket standing by to catch any left over water in the pump hoses, and remove them from the pump. The pump is held on to the motor by two spring clips. (Figure DD-4) Remove the

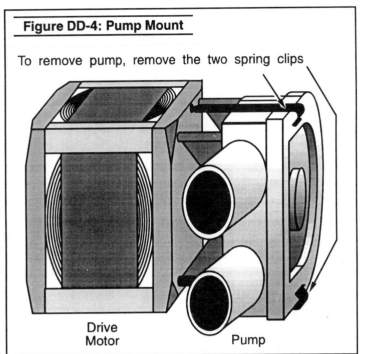

Figure DD-4: Pump Mount

To remove pump, remove the two spring clips

Drive Motor

Pump

spring clips and pull the pump off the motor shaft.

When replacing the pump, make sure you check the pump discharge hose for any impeller pieces that may be clogging it. Also, when installing the hose clamps, put them in a position where they won't hit the cabinet when the machine wobbles off-balance.

4-5 AGITATOR

The agitator is held to the driveshaft by a bolt. To get to it, remove any softener dispenser by pulling it straight off. Remove the agitator cap by pulling or prying off with a screwdriver (depending on what kind you have; see Figure DD-5.) Remove the center bolt and tug straight up on the agitator skirt to remove. If you have trouble removing the bolt, see section 3-8 in Chapter 3.

Inspect the spline of the shaft and the agitator for wear. If the agitator is slipping on the agitator driveshaft spline, replace it.

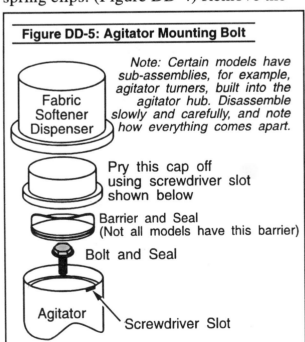

Figure DD-5: Agitator Mounting Bolt

Fabric Softener Dispenser

Note: Certain models have sub-assemblies, for example, agitator turners, built into the agitator hub. Disassemble slowly and carefully, and note how everything comes apart.

Pry this cap off using screwdriver slot shown below

Barrier and Seal (Not all models have this barrier)

Bolt and Seal

Agitator

Screwdriver Slot

4-6 BASKET SERVICE

The direct drive washer uses a unique liquid balancing system built into the basket. Around the top of the basket is a "ballast" compartment which is filled with a special liquid. When the basket spins, the liquid inside this compartment moves around to dampen any imbalance present. Remove the basket to inspect this ballast compartment.

Removal of the basket requires a special spanner tool, available inexpensively from your parts dealer.

First, remove the tub ring from the top of the tub (Figure DD-6) and the agitator (Section 4-5.)

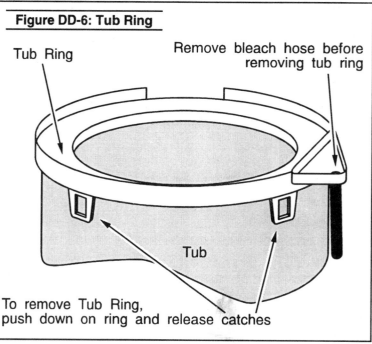

Figure DD-6: Tub Ring

Tub Ring

Remove bleach hose before removing tub ring

Tub

To remove Tub Ring, push down on ring and release catches

Next, remove the fill line vacuum break by squeezing the plastic mounting tabs together, and pulling outward and downward. (Figure DD-7.)

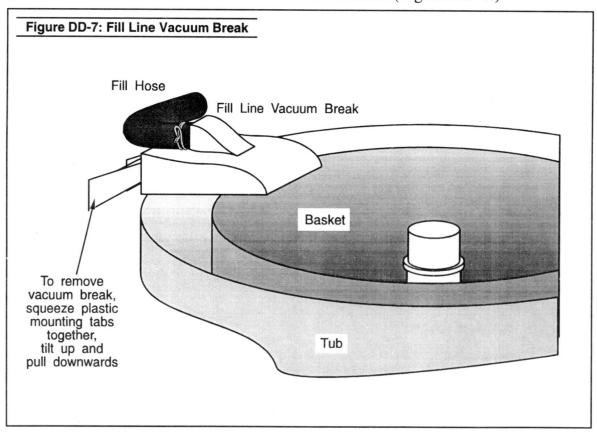

Figure DD-7: Fill Line Vacuum Break

Fill Hose

Fill Line Vacuum Break

Basket

To remove vacuum break, squeeze plastic mounting tabs together, tilt up and pull downwards

Tub

Now, using the special tool, remove the spanner nut from the centerpost. (Figure DD-8) If you need to tap on the spanner to remove the nut, be careful not to hit the porcelain interior of the basket. It will chip.

On the outside of the basket near the top, there will be a fill hole which is plugged up. If the hole is leaking, the basket must be replaced. The balancing ballast compartment cannot be serviced.

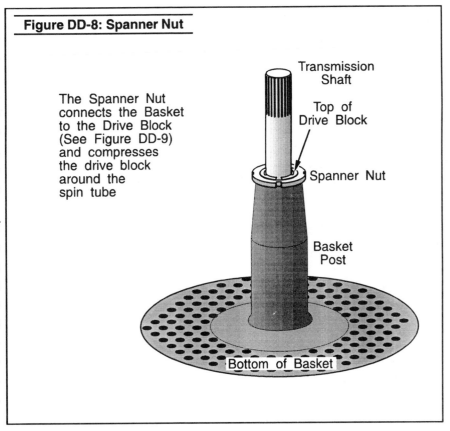

Figure DD-8: Spanner Nut

The Spanner Nut connects the Basket to the Drive Block (See Figure DD-9) and compresses the drive block around the spin tube

Transmission Shaft

Top of Drive Block

Spanner Nut

Basket Post

Bottom of Basket

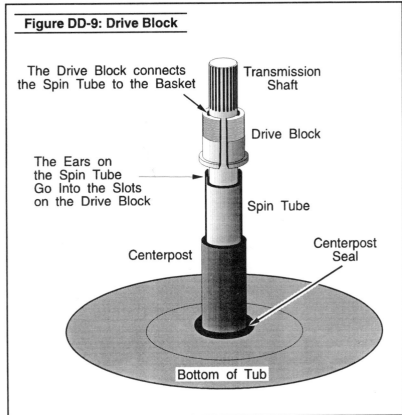

Figure DD-9: Drive Block

The Drive Block connects the Spin Tube to the Basket

Transmission Shaft

Drive Block

The Ears on the Spin Tube Go Into the Slots on the Drive Block

Spin Tube

Centerpost

Centerpost Seal

Bottom of Tub

4-7 REMOVING THE TUB

Remove the agitator and basket as described in sections 4-5 and 4-6.

Remove the drive block by tapping upwards on the underside of it with a hammer. (Figure DD-9)

CAUTION: *the metal of the drive block is soft, so don't tap too hard, or you may damage it.*

Remove the water level switch hose and the tub drain hose from the tub. Have a bucket standing by to catch any leftover water in the drain hose.

Disconnect the pump hose and water level pressure switch hose from the tub. Some water may come out, so be prepared.

Remove the three suspension springs from the tub suspension brackets (figure DD-10) There will be a fourth, counterweight spring attached to either the left front bracket or the center rear bracket. Remove it.

CAUTION: Mark all brackets and springs to be sure you get them back on the washer in exactly the same place.

Remove the brackets from the tub.

Scrape any soap deposits off the centerpost, and lubricate it with some liquid soap so the tub will slide off easily. Pull the tub straight up and off the centerpost.

To replace the centerpost seal, squeeze it from inside the tub and push it through the bottom of the tub to the outside.

Re-assembly is the opposite of disassembly. Make sure all springs and brackets are in their original places. If any springs are broken, replace all *four* as a set.

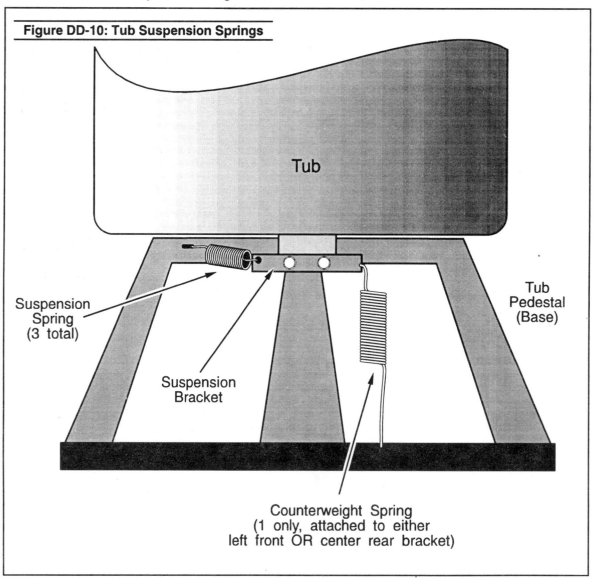

Figure DD-10: Tub Suspension Springs

Tub

Suspension
Spring
(3 total)

Suspension
Bracket

Tub
Pedestal
(Base)

Counterweight Spring
(1 only, attached to either
left front OR center rear bracket)

4-8 MOTOR AND COUPLING

These machines have an external capacitor located in the console, not anywhere near the motor. To find it, open the console as described in section 4-2 and look inside the left side of the console. Before handling the motor, you must discharge and test the capacitor as described in section 2-5(e).

The motor coupling will break if the transmission locks up while the machine is running. It simply presses on to both the motor and transmission shafts. (Figure DD-11)

Do make sure the machine is unplugged before removing the motor.

If the motor is humming but not turning, remove it from the transmission as follows: (Figure DD-11.)

Disconnect power and remove the cabinet. (Section 4-2)

Following the safety precautions in section 1-5(4), lay the washer on its back and remove the two screws holding the bottom panel in place. Remove the bottom panel.

Remove the two spring clips holding the pump to the motor. No need to remove the pump hoses; just slide the pump off the motor shaft.

There may be two motor harness connectors, or only one. Disconnect it (them).

Two spring clips hold the motor to the transmission. (Figure DD-11) There may be screws holding the spring clips on; these are put on for shipping, and need not be re-installed. Remove the spring clips, and the motor will slide off.

Try turning the transmission by hand, in both directions. If it will not turn, it is locked up. Replace it as described in section 4-9. If it does turn easily, then either the starting switch or motor is bad. Test and repair as described in section 2-5(e).

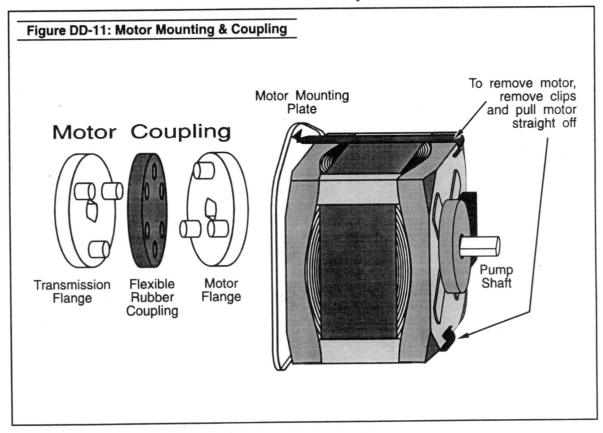

Figure DD-11: Motor Mounting & Coupling

Motor Coupling

Transmission Flange

Flexible Rubber Coupling

Motor Flange

Motor Mounting Plate

To remove motor, remove clips and pull motor straight off

Pump Shaft

4-9 TRANSMISSION

Removal of the transmission is a relatively simple matter in these machines.

Remove the agitator, basket and drive block. (Section 4-5, 4-6 & 4-7) No need to remove the tub; just the drive block.

Lay the washer on its back and remove the two screws holding the bottom panel in place. Remove the bottom panel.

Remove the two spring clips holding the pump to the motor. No need to remove the pump hoses; just slide the pump off the motor shaft.

There may be two motor wiring harness connectors, or only one. Disconnect it (or them).

Remove the three transmission mounting bolts (Figure DD-12) and slowly pull the transmission straight out.

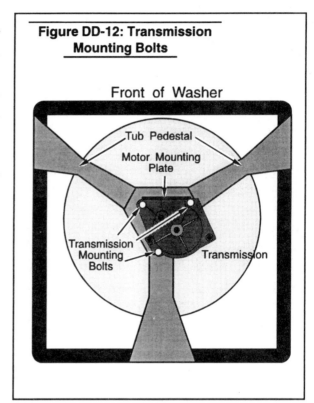

Figure DD-12: Transmission Mounting Bolts

Front of Washer

Tub Pedestal

Motor Mounting Plate

Transmission Mounting Bolts

Transmission

Installation is the opposite of removal. Be sure the motor coupling sticks out in the same direction as it did when you pulled the tranny off.

4-10 CLUTCH AND BRAKE

To service the clutch or brake, you must remove the transmission as described in section 4-9.

When you have removed the transmission, look on top of it for the clutch drum. (Figure DD-13) The clutch shoes can be removed simply by squeezing the spring with a pair of pliers. Check for a broken clutch spring or a worn clutch lining.

Figure DD-13: Clutch Assembly

To remove clutch lining: Squeeze clutch spring with pliers

Agitator Shaft

UP

Clutch Drum

Clutch Lining

When re-installing, tab must stick upwards

The brake and spin tube assembly is still attached to the tub pedestal. (Figure DD-14) To remove the spin tube assembly, turn the release cam counterclockwise and pull the spin tube straight out.

Inspect the spin tube for scoring. Also inspect the brake spring for breakage and the shoes for wear. Replace the whole assembly if defective.

To re-install the spin tube, go slowly and be careful not to catch or gouge any seals or bearings.

4-11 TIMER

The timer can be removed by holding the timer dial while turning the timer knob to the left. The timer dial will then lift off a "D" shaped shaft, to reveal the timer mounting screws. (Figure DD-15.)

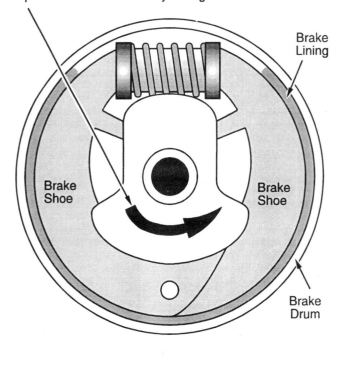

Figure DD-14: Spin Tube Assembly Removal

To remove brake and spin tube assembly:
Twist the hub counter-clockwise to relieve brake tension and pull the whole assembly straight out

Brake Lining

Brake Shoe

Brake Shoe

Brake Drum

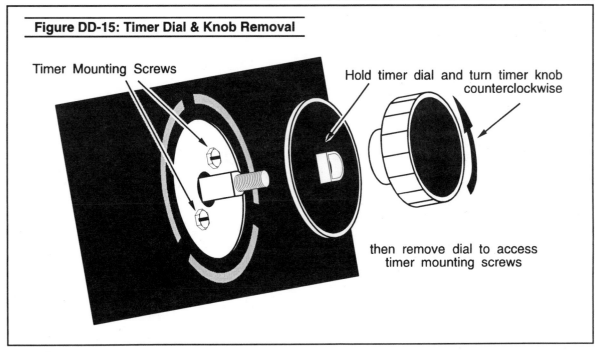

Figure DD-15: Timer Dial & Knob Removal

Timer Mounting Screws

Hold timer dial and turn timer knob counterclockwise

then remove dial to access timer mounting screws

Chapter 5

OLD-STYLE GENERAL ELECTRIC
including Hotpoint & JC Penney

5-1 BASIC OPERATION

The old-style GE design uses a single-speed reversing motor, which is belted to the transmission. When viewed from the top, the motor turns clockwise for the agitation cycle, and counterclockwise for the spin cycle (Figure GE-1.)

A simple centrifugal clutch prevents the motor from taking heavy shock loads when starting. Some models have a two-speed clutch (only the clutch is two-speed, not the motor.) The second speed is slower, for "gentle" cycles, and is solenoid-activated.

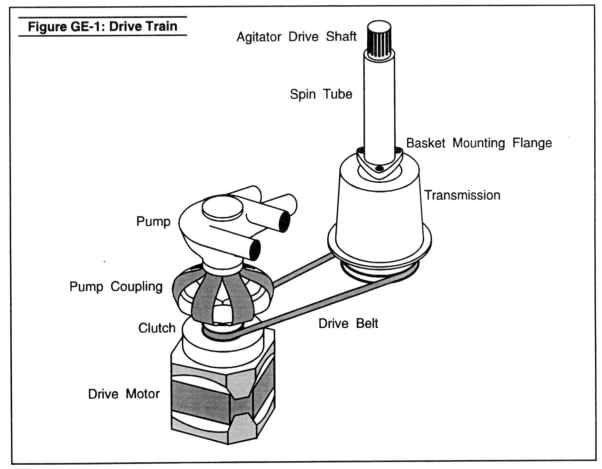

Figure GE-1: Drive Train

Agitator Drive Shaft

Spin Tube

Basket Mounting Flange

Transmission

Pump

Pump Coupling

Clutch

Drive Belt

Drive Motor

The pump is also direct-reversing. It is connected directly to the motor through a flexible coupling. Most GE pumps have two impellers and four hose connections. One impeller recirculates water during the wash and rinse cycles, and the other pumps water out of the tub during the spin cycle.

5-2 OPENING THE CABINET AND CONSOLE

See Figure GE-2 for details about opening the cabinet and console.

In raising the top of the cabinet, you must keep two things in mind:

1) It is better to use a putty knife, rather than a screwdriver, to push the catches. There is less chance of chipping or scratching the finish.

2) Inside the lid, on the top right side, is the recirculation nozzle. (see figure GE-7) The nozzle fits through a hole in the soft plastic skirt attached to the top of the cabinet. You must push the nozzle out of the skirt as you raise the cabinet top, and insert the nozzle back through the skirt when you lower it.

Most GE machines have a wiring diagram in an envelope inside the console.

5-3 DIAGNOSIS

Since the operating system is so simple, the easiest way to diagnose a mechanical problem is to open up the back of the washer and observe things while you run the washer through its cycles. Following are the most common problems:

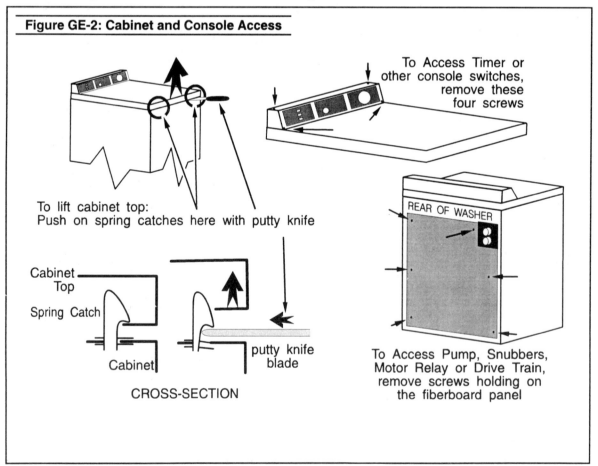

Figure GE-2: Cabinet and Console Access

To Access Timer or other console switches, remove these four screws

To lift cabinet top:
Push on spring catches here with putty knife

Cabinet Top

Spring Catch

Cabinet

putty knife blade

CROSS-SECTION

REAR OF WASHER

To Access Pump, Snubbers, Motor Relay or Drive Train, remove screws holding on the fiberboard panel

DIAGNOSIS 1: WATER LEAKS.

See section 2-6 on leaks and backed up drains.

Besides the usual loose or worn hoses and fill system problems, leaks in these washers most commonly come from one of five places:

1) Look at the pump through the back of the washer. There is a tiny inspection hole in the pump body that weeps water when the pump's internal seal is leaking. You may not see any water directly, but you will see its tracks leading down the pump body. See section 5-4 on pumps.

2) These washers are quite different from others in that the tub is attached to the cabinet, rather than the transmission. If there is an imbalance, only the basket and drive train wobbles; not the whole tub. (See Figure GE-3)

Between the transmission and tub, there is a large flexible rubber seal called a boot. This boot can get brittle and crusted with detergent. It can develop leaks, or even shake loose, causing a MASSIVE leak (during the fill cycle, the water dumps straight onto the floor instead of filling the tub). Look for water coming from around the top of the transmission. See section 5-6.

3) Since the basket is free to move around in the tub, the basket may hit the tub if there is too large an imbalance. If this happens too often, it can actually wear a hole in the tub. Usually such holes will appear around the top of the tub. If you have holes worn in the tub, you can sometimes patch them with an epoxy patch kit, available at your appliance parts dealer. It may prove to be a temporary repair, but you can always do it again, and it's cheaper than trashing the washer. I've also recently discovered an excellent new product called Slapstix. It is a plastic abrasion-resistant patch kit made specifically for GE washers. As of this writing, it is not yet widely available, but ask your dealer or call 800-936-5282.

4) The tub fittings may leak. If you detect a leak from the tub drain or other tub fitting, remove the basket as described in section 5-6.

5) You may get a calcium or detergent buildup around the fill or recirculation nozzle. Such a buildup can cause the nozzle to spray water over the top of the tub. Clean out or replace the nozzle.

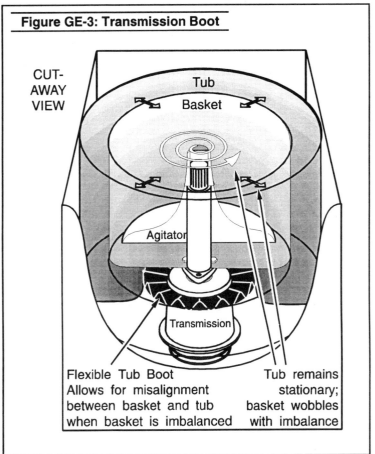

Figure GE-3: Transmission Boot

CUT-AWAY VIEW

Tub
Basket
Agitator
Transmission

Flexible Tub Boot
Allows for misalignment
between basket and tub
when basket is imbalanced

Tub remains
stationary;
basket wobbles
with imbalance

DIAGNOSIS 2: BASKET SPINS, BUT WATER DOESN'T DRAIN FROM TUB.

Usually the pump has gone belly up. Replace it as described in section 5-4.

If the machine is not pumping out water because the coupling has come off the pump, check the pump for jamming. See section 5-4.

DIAGNOSIS 3: SLOW OR NO AGITATE AND/OR SPIN.

When diagnosing this problem, keep in mind that the pump is coupled directly to the motor; it does not receive power through the clutch. Only the transmission receives power through the clutch and belt. Therefore, a locked transmission *will not* stop the motor from turning, but a locked pump *will*.

1) If NOTHING on the machine works, and it's not even making any noise, check the power supply. Also check the electrical components in section 2-5.

NOTE: In some models, the lid switch stops the machine completely. In others, only the spin cycle is interlocked, and the machine will still fill and agitate with the lid raised. Check your wiring diagram.

2) The belt may be broken or loose. Check as described in section 2-4(a) and tighten or replace as described in section 5-10.

3) Often a sock or something has jammed in the pump. This symptom is often accompanied by a strong burning smell. You will also hear the motor trying to start, then tripping off by the motor overload switch, because it is being stalled by the pump. An additional confirmation of this diagnosis is that if you look at the pump coupling while the motor is trying to start, it will be twisted tightly. See section 5-4.

4) If the transmission pulley is turning, but either agitate or spin or both are not working, the transmission is bad. Replace as described in section 5-13.

If the pump is turning, but the transmission drive pulley is not turning, stop the washer and disconnect power. Try turning the transmission pulley by hand, in both directions. If the transmission pulley will not turn in one or both directions, the transmission needs to be replaced. See section 5-13.

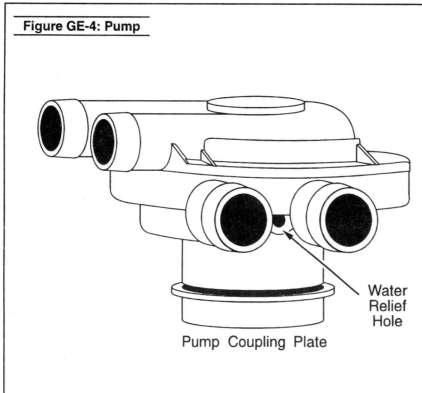

Figure GE-4: Pump

Water Relief Hole

Pump Coupling Plate

If the transmission pulley turns fairly easily by hand, but the clutch drum is turning slowly or not at all under motor power, the clutch may be bad. Usually there will be a loud rattling noise. See section 5-11.

5) The motor or starting solenoid may be burnt out. Remember that the motor *may* start in one direction, but not in the other. Usually you will hear the motor buzzing as it tries to start, then dropping out on the overload. Check as described in section 5-12.

6) If the washer spins but does not agitate, check the agitator splines. Section 5-5.

7) If you have a two-speed machine and the slow (gentle) speed is not working, the clutch solenoid may not be working. See section 5-11.

DIAGNOSIS 4: BASKET SPINS (CLOCKWISE) WHILE AGITATING.

The transmission needs to be replaced. See section 5-13.

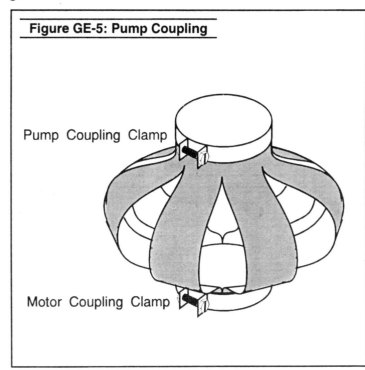

Figure GE-5: Pump Coupling

Pump Coupling Clamp

Motor Coupling Clamp

DIAGNOSIS 5: OIL LEAKS.

A little bit of oil leakage is normal. If oil is leaking so badly that it is slinging off the transmission drive pulley and getting around the inside of the cabinet, you will need to replace the transmission as described in section 5-13.

DIAGNOSIS 6: EXCESSIVE NOISE OR VIBRATION

A whining or loud clattering noise is usually a worn clutch. See section 5-11.

If the machine makes a squeaking noise, especially during the spin cycle, the snubbers are probably worn out. This is especially true if the machine has difficulty balancing during spin, even after you redistribute the clothes. Replace the snubber blocks as described in section 5-14.

5-4 PUMP AND PUMP COUPLING

A vast majority of GE-built washers use the pump shown in figure GE-4. A few less-expensive models used a non-recirculating pump with only two hose connections.

The pump is connected directly to the motor through a rubber/fabric flexible coupling (Figure GE-5.) The pump coupling is connected to both by a round clamp at each end. When installing a new coupling, do not remove the staples that hold it in shape. Also, put the gaps in the clamps directly over the gaps in the coupling.

If the pump seal is leaking, you will see water weeping (or the tracks of a water weep) from the hole shown in figure GE-4.

There are no special tricks to replacing a GE pump. First, drain the tub as described in section 1-6. Disconnect the pump coupling at the TOP end, then the remove the three pump mounting screws. Have a bucket ready to catch water, and remove the four pump hoses.

Installation is the opposite of removal.

If something is jamming the pump, the pump coupling will be twisted tightly while the motor is trying to start. Check for jams as described in section 2-3.

If the pump is not turning freely, but you cannot find a jam, replace the pump.

If the coupling has come off the pump, make sure you check that the pump is turning freely.

5-5 AGITATOR

Most GE-designed agitators are not fastened to the shaft by any screws or bolts. To remove, simply tug upwards on the bottom of the agitator. There are exceptions; see "handwash" agitators below.

If you find that you cannot remove the agitator by pulling on it, try tapping the top of the agitator gently with a rubber or wooden mallet. If you *still* cannot remove the agitator, pry off the plastic cap in the center. Then cut out the little piece of plastic in the center of the hub with a knife; this will expose the top of the agitator shaft. (Figure GE-6) Hit it with a little WD-40 to loosen it.

GE-designed agitators have a removable rubber spline insert that connects the agitator to the transmission shaft splines (Figure GE-6.) If the splines are stripped, you can replace the whole agitator, or just the rubber spline insert.

To remove the insert, remove the plastic cap and cut out the center plastic piece as described above. Push out the old spline insert (it can be difficult.) To replace, put the new insert onto the top of the transmission shaft and push the agitator down onto it.

Hotpoint and JC Penney have a "handwash" agitator on some designs. The "handwash" agitator is actually a small agitator that fits inside the larger, main agitator. The "handwash" agitator has a small screw underneath the metal disc on top of the agitator; make sure you remove it

Figure GE-6: Agitator Hub

To remove a stuck agitator, Pry off cap and (in some models) cut out center piece.

Rubber Spline Insert connects Agitator Shaft to Agitator

before trying to pull up on the "handwash" agitator. There are locking tabs that you must twist to remove the larger agitator from the smaller one.

Once the screw is removed, the "handwash" agitator should lift out easily. If not, tap with a rubber mallet a described above, or shoot some WD-40 into the screw hole.

5-6 TUB BOOT SEAL AND TUB FITTINGS

To access the transmission boot or replace tub fittings, you must remove the basket.

Drain the tub, raise the cabinet top, and remove the agitator as described in section 5-5. Remove the recirculation nozzle (figure GE-7) by simply pulling it straight out. Remove the agitator bushing by pressing on the spring-loaded tab. Beneath the agitator bushing are three basket mounting bolts. (Figure GE-8.) Remove the three bolts with a 1/2-inch 12-point socket or box wrench and lift out the basket.

Figure GE-7: Recirculation Nozzle Removal

To remove recirculation nozzle, pull it straight out of its rubber mount

Tub

Basket

Agitator

VIEW:
Front of Washer
Cabinet Top Raised

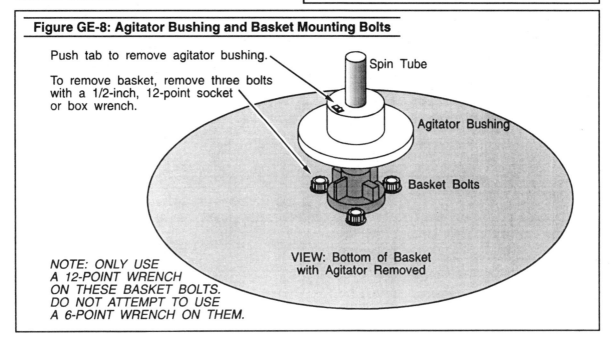

Figure GE-8: Agitator Bushing and Basket Mounting Bolts

Push tab to remove agitator bushing.

To remove basket, remove three bolts with a 1/2-inch, 12-point socket or box wrench.

Spin Tube

Agitator Bushing

Basket Bolts

VIEW: Bottom of Basket with Agitator Removed

NOTE: ONLY USE A 12-POINT WRENCH ON THESE BASKET BOLTS. DO NOT ATTEMPT TO USE A 6-POINT WRENCH ON THEM.

The tub boot and all tub fittings will now be visible. (Figure GE-9) IF THE TUB BOOT IS NOT LEAKING, DO NOT REMOVE IT. If you need to remove it, it is simply clamped to the transmission top and to a lip on the tub by two big round clamps. If it has simply shaken loose and not torn, you can just clamp the old one back in place, but you'd better check the snubber blocks as described in section 5-14 to try to find out why it shook loose in the first place.

Re-assembly is the opposite of disassembly.

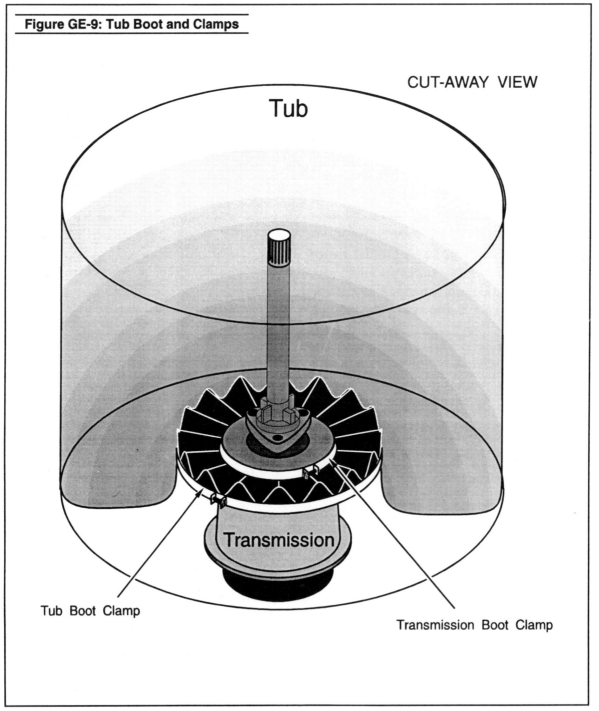

Figure GE-9: Tub Boot and Clamps

CUT-AWAY VIEW

Tub

Transmission

Tub Boot Clamp

Transmission Boot Clamp

5-7 TIMER

Testing the timer is described in section 2-5(c).

To test or remove the timer, remove the console as described in section 5-2. If the timer dial prevents you from removing the timer, pull off the spring clip from behind the timer knob as shown in figure GE-10. Mark the timer wires as you remove them, or better yet, pull the wires off the old timer and put them directly on the new one, one at a time.

GE used two basic timer designs over the years. One used a metal housing. The other design is known as a "clamshell" timer because of the shape of its plastic housing. Both are rebuildable, though not by a novice. If your timer is defective, take it to your parts dealer and ask for a rebuilt.

Figure GE-10: Timer Dial Spring Clip

To remove timer knob, remove spring clip from behind it with a pair of needlenose pliers

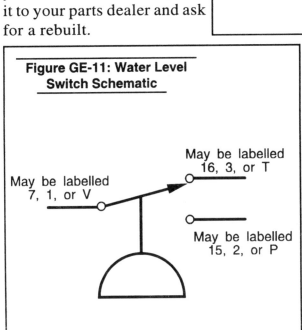
Figure GE-11: Water Level Switch Schematic

May be labelled 16, 3, or T

May be labelled 7, 1, or V

May be labelled 15, 2, or P

5-8 LID SWITCH

The lid switch is located beneath the cabinet top, towards the right rear of the washer. It is a simple, mechanically-activated switch. Test with an ohmmeter and replace if defective.

5-9 WATER LEVEL SWITCH

The water level switch is located beneath the console. GE washers used several different wiring schemes, so refer to section 2-5(b) and compare with figure GE-11 to determine which terminals to test. If the switch is bad, replace it.

5-10 BELT

Remove power from the washer and remove the back panel as described in section 5-2.

To tension the belt, loosen the three motor mounting bolts on the underside of the motor mounting plate. Proper tension is when the belt can be deflected approximately 1/2-inch, midway between the motor and transmission pulleys, with your fingers. Use your hands; you do not need any extra leverage on the motor to set proper belt tension.

To replace the belt, simply remove the upper pump coupling and install the new belt.

5-11 CLUTCH

GE washers use two different clutches (Figure GE-12.)

The two-speed clutch can be identified by the solenoid that activates the slow speed. It also has a larger outer clutch drum. If the slow (gentle) agitator speed is not working, test the solenoid coil for continuity. If it has no continuity, replace by removing the screw on the underside of the coil.

I do not recommend the novice trying to rebuild a two-speed clutch. They are complex assemblies; difficult to disassemble, assemble, and adjust. If you suspect your two-speed clutch assembly is

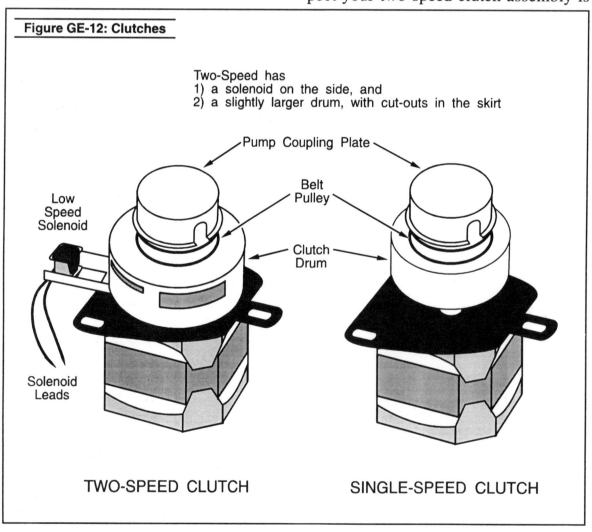

Figure GE-12: Clutches

Two-Speed has
1) a solenoid on the side, and
2) a slightly larger drum, with cut-outs in the skirt

Pump Coupling Plate

Belt Pulley

Low Speed Solenoid

Clutch Drum

Solenoid Leads

TWO-SPEED CLUTCH   SINGLE-SPEED CLUTCH

bad, remove the motor and clutch assembly from the machine and take the assembly to a rebuilder.

On the other hand, a single-speed clutch is a relatively simple assembly. To service the single-speed clutch, first remove power from the washer and remove the back panel. Disconnect the pump coupling, loosen the motor mounting bolts, and remove the drive belt. Disconnect the motor wiring at the terminal block. Remove the motor mounting bolts (be careful; the motor is heavy!) and remove the motor and clutch assembly from the washer.

Figure GE-13: Pump Coupling Plate Removal

Pump Coupling Plate

Motor Shaft Extension

Clutch Drum

Roll Pin

Using a straight punch, drive the roll pin out of the motor shaft extension. You can then easily lift off the pump coupling plate.

There is a roll pin in the pump coupling plate on top of the clutch pulley. Drive it out with a straight punch. (Figure GE-13.) Lift off the pump coupling plate.

Lift off the clutch drum. If it does not lift off easily, tap lightly on the motor shaft extension with a hammer. If that doesn't get it off, you will need to use a wheel puller and horseshoe collar.

CAUTION: If you use a wheel puller to remove the clutch drum, do not pull on the skirt of the drum. Use a horseshoe collar (Figure GE-14) to pull on the drive pulley.

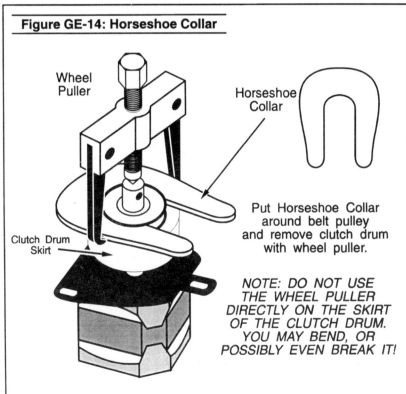

Figure GE-14: Horseshoe Collar

Wheel Puller

Horseshoe Collar

Clutch Drum Skirt

Put Horseshoe Collar around belt pulley and remove clutch drum with wheel puller.

NOTE: DO NOT USE THE WHEEL PULLER DIRECTLY ON THE SKIRT OF THE CLUTCH DRUM. YOU MAY BEND, OR POSSIBLY EVEN BREAK IT!

See figure GE-15 for disassembly of the clutch components. Inspect the shoes and clutch drum for excessive wear. If you're not sure if the shoes can be re-used, ask your appliance parts dealer, or simply replace them. They're cheap insurance against future problems.

Normally you will not need to remove the shaft extension, but do inspect it, and replace if worn or damaged.

Reassembly is the opposite of disassembly. To get the roll pin in, line up the holes and stick in a nail to keep the holes aligned. Then drive the pin in from the opposite side as the nail.

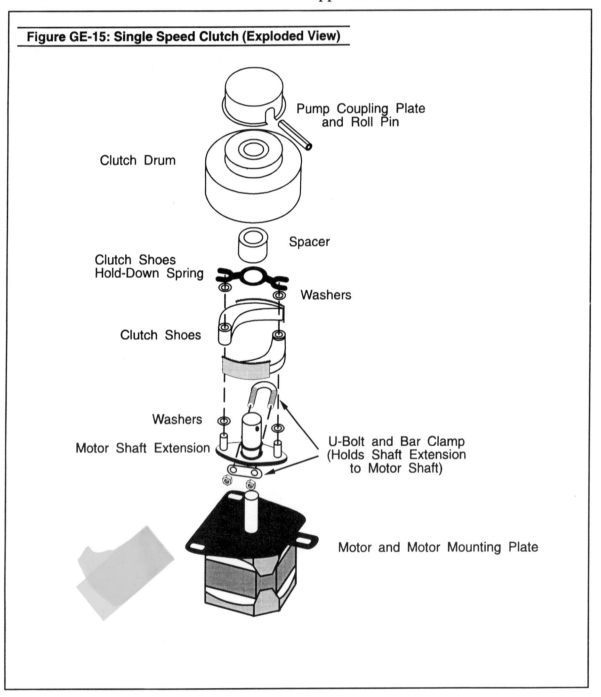

Figure GE-15: Single Speed Clutch (Exploded View)

Pump Coupling Plate and Roll Pin

Clutch Drum

Spacer

Clutch Shoes Hold-Down Spring

Washers

Clutch Shoes

Washers

Motor Shaft Extension

U-Bolt and Bar Clamp (Holds Shaft Extension to Motor Shaft)

Motor and Motor Mounting Plate

5-12 MOTOR AND RELAY

If you hear the motor trying to start, but dropping out on the motor overload, and the pump coupling is not twisted when the motor is trying to start, either the relay is defective or a motor winding is burnt out. Test as described below.

RELAY

GE washers use a separate relay. Remove the back panel. As you look at the back of the machine, you will find the relay towards the upper left side of the machine. (Figure GE-16)

To test the relay, first remove power from the machine. Mark the relay wires and remove them. Remove the relay from the machine.

With your ohmmeter set on Rx1, test between the terminals marked "M" and "LS." You should see *good* continuity.

Test between the terminals marked "L" and "S." You should see *no* continuity.

Turn the relay *UPSIDE DOWN* and test again between the "L" and "S" terminals. You should now see *good* continuity.

If you do not get the above readings, replace the relay. It is very important to get the right relay; it matches the motor that's installed.

MOTOR

If the relay is not bad, the motor is. Replace the motor and relay as a pair. Make sure you get the right motor for your machine. The motor mount is held in place by three nuts.

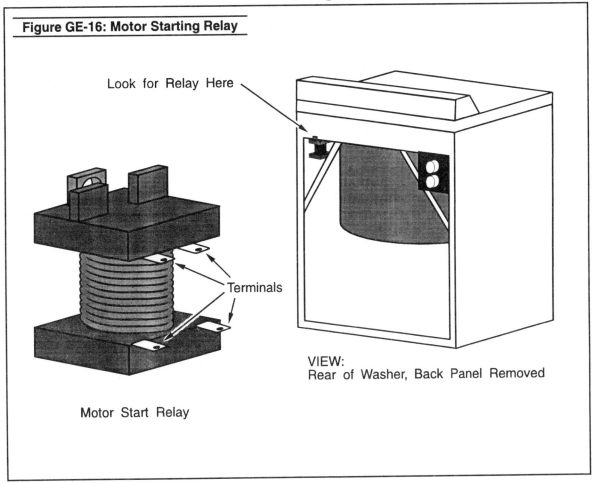

Figure GE-16: Motor Starting Relay

Look for Relay Here

Terminals

Motor Start Relay

VIEW:
Rear of Washer, Back Panel Removed

5-13 TRANSMISSION

To replace the transmission, first remove the basket and tub boot as described in section 5-6.

Remove the six transmission mounting bolts shown in figure GE-17. Slide the transmission towards the right rear of the washer, and reach under the transmission to make sure the drive belt has disengaged from it. Lift out the transmission (be careful; it is heavy.)

The transmission can be rebuilt, but not by the novice. Rebuilt GE transmissions are a standard item at most parts stores, and they are not terribly expensive. Make sure you get the right shaft length.

Replacement is the opposite of removal. Lower the transmission into place, and slip the drive belt on. Locate the right rear bolt loosely in its hole, then the left front bolt, then the other four.

Install the boot, basket, and agitator. As a final step, remove the back from the washer and make sure the belt is seated properly.

Figure GE-17: Transmission Mounting Bolts

VIEW:
Bottom of Tub
Tub Boot Removed

Slide Transmission towards the right rear of the machine (to disengage drive belt) and lift it out.

Remove these three transmission mounting bolts and the three on the back side of the transmission

BE CAREFUL LIFTING THE TRANSMISSION! IT IS HEAVY!

5-14 SNUBBER BLOCKS

There are eight friction pads, commonly known as snubber blocks, which help to prevent vibration during the spin cycle. There are two in each corner of the machine. (Figure GE-18) These can wear out, causing excessive vibration and a squeaking noise. Often they will be missing when you look for them. Lift the spring and replace them. Be careful not to catch your fingers under the spring.

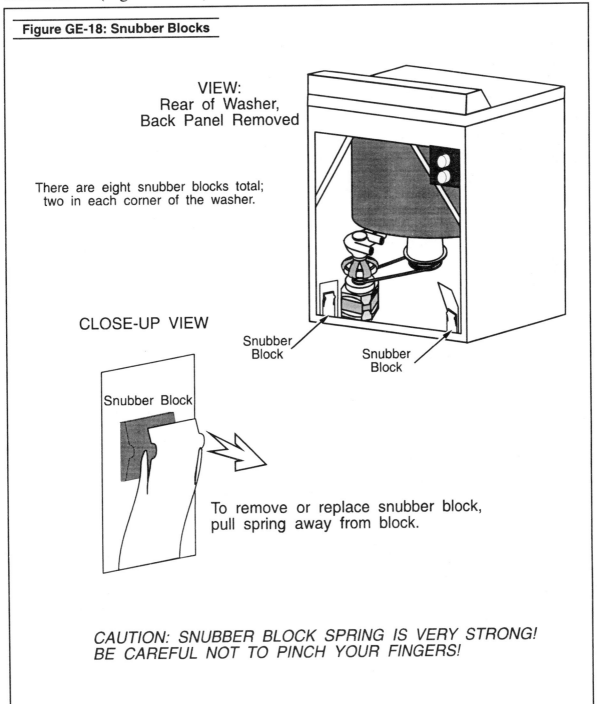

Figure GE-18: Snubber Blocks

VIEW:
Rear of Washer,
Back Panel Removed

There are eight snubber blocks total; two in each corner of the washer.

Snubber Block

Snubber Block

CLOSE-UP VIEW

Snubber Block

To remove or replace snubber block, pull spring away from block.

CAUTION: SNUBBER BLOCK SPRING IS VERY STRONG! BE CAREFUL NOT TO PINCH YOUR FINGERS!

Chapter 6

GE FRONT-ACCESS MACHINES
including Hotpoint, JC Penney & RCA

In 1995, GE began manufacturing a new washing machine. They are commonly referred to as the "front-access" or "easy-access" machines, or simply the "new-style" GE washer, versus the "old-style" machine. GE sells them under several brands and model names, including "Profile" and "Maxus."

The jury is still out on the long-term quality and reliability of these machines. There are a few quirks and problems starting to show up. However, except for the drain hose, everything is easily serviceable from the front of the machine as advertised.

6-1 OPERATING SYSTEM

These machines are direct-reversing. The drive motor drives the transmission through a clutch and a belt. The belt is the same one used in the old machine.

The basket is attached directly to the transmission, which itself spins during the spin cycle. When the motor stops or reverses, a brake attached to the bottom of the transmission engages, keeping the transmission from turning during agitation. (Figure FA-1)

There is no pump-driven water recirculation. Flexible fins on the agitator circulate water in the tub and through the self-cleaning lint filter in the basket hub.

One of the unique features is that the drive motor does not drive the pump. The drain pump in these machines is a separate unit with its' own motor.

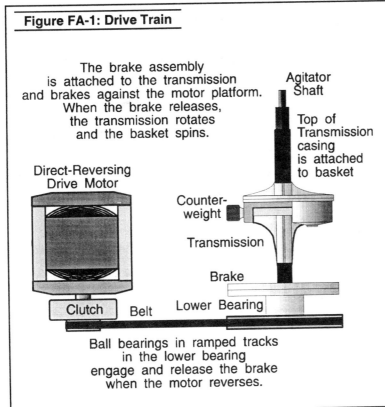

Figure FA-1: Drive Train

The brake assembly is attached to the transmission and brakes against the motor platform. When the brake releases, the transmission rotates and the basket spins.

Direct-Reversing Drive Motor

Clutch   Belt

Agitator Shaft

Top of Transmission casing is attached to basket

Counter-weight

Transmission

Brake

Lower Bearing

Ball bearings in ramped tracks in the lower bearing engage and release the brake when the motor reverses.

The suspension in these machines is reported to be VERY good. In one videotaped demo I saw, they put eight pounds of phone books in the machine during the spin cycle and the thing barely vibrated. In fact, if the washer is dancing around during the spin cycle, whoever installed the machine probably forgot to remove the suspension rod, inserted to keep the tub from moving during shipping. (It's a long rod, almost the width of the machine, that you pull out of a hole on the bottom right side of the cabinet.) The suspension system is supplemented by a liquid-filled (unserviceable) balance ring in the top of the basket.

Some customers have complained about the pump being too loud. On the higher-end models, GE put some sound deadening insulation in the cabinet, but if you don't have one of these machines, there is an insulation kit available with panels that stick on the inside of the cabinet.

A few more tidbits of info about these machines:

1) All functions are interlocked through the lid switch except the fill cycle. The washer will not agitate, drain or spin with the lid open.

2) There is a pre-pump function built into the water level switch. The water level must be quite low before the water level switch will allow the basket to start spinning.

Most of the parts on these machines are designed to be thrown away. For example, the transmission is a tiny little thing that was designed in large part around EPA requirements (less than 3 ounces of oil, stuff like that.) It was NOT designed with rebuilding in mind.

6-2 SYMPTOMS

A very common problem with these machines is that the drain hose, which is made of plastic instead of rubber, cracks and leaks. The triangle bracket that holds it on is a separate item and is very difficult to get off the hose. Replace the hose and the triangle bracket with it. (Figure FA-2)

They have also been experiencing some drain pump leaks and failures. The fan blades on the front of the pump should turn easily by hand. If not, check for something jamming the pump. If it turns easily by hand but won't drain the tub, replace the whole pump and motor assembly. Ditto if the pump leaks. See section 6-4.

Another early problem experienced with these machines is with a bleach dispenser / hose installed only on two-speed machines. Besides the fact that bleach is very hard on plastic and rubber parts, such as the hose itself, the hose

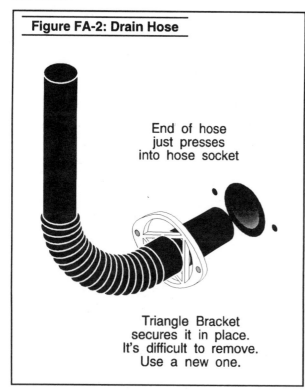

Figure FA-2: Drain Hose

End of hose just presses into hose socket

Triangle Bracket secures it in place. It's difficult to remove. Use a new one.

chafes on one of the suspension rods until a hole develops. (Figure FA-3) Bleach then dribbles out and directly onto the drive motor connectors. The symptom is that the drive motor hums and will not start. There is a replacement wiring harness available; try that first. If the drive motor still won't start, it may need to be replaced. See section 6-4. Incidentally, you won't see this except in the earliest models; when this problem started showing up, GE quickly redesigned the bleach dispenser hose routing.

Another common complaint is that water leaks during the agitate cycle. What is happening is that the lower transmission ball bearings are worn so the brake is not engaging fully. The basket then spins during the agitate cycle and and slings water over the edge of the tub. The basket obviously will not brake properly at the end of the spin cycle either. A lower bearing kit is available to rebuild the lower (ball) bearing assembly. See section 6-5.

The clutches have been experiencing some failures. The problem here is that the clutch pulley is pressed together and the top half of it comes off. You'll find the belt and the top half of the pulley just laying there. Obviously the machine does not agitate or spin.

Another problem experienced, though it doesn't appear to be a widespread problem yet, is that there have been some transmission failures. The symp-

tom is that you attempt to remove the agitator, and the whole agitator shaft comes out with it. A spring clip inside is coming loose. Replace the whole transmission and brake assembly as described in section 6-5.

If you think water may be leaking from the seal between the tub and transmission, see section 6-5.

6-3 CONSOLE

To access the timer, temperature or water level switches, fill valve, or to remove the cabinet top, you must remove the console. Remove the four #15 torx-head screws on top and the console drops off. You can then pull the terminal blocks off the timer and any other switches in the console and set it aside.

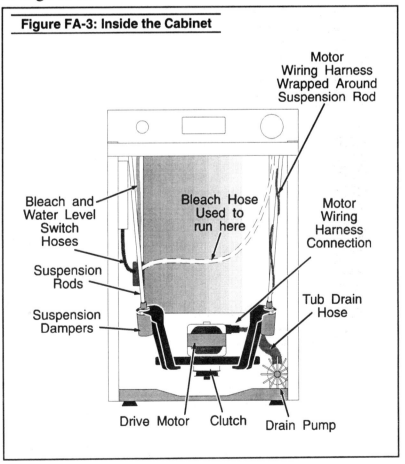

Figure FA-3: Inside the Cabinet

Motor Wiring Harness Wrapped Around Suspension Rod

Bleach and Water Level Switch Hoses

Bleach Hose Used to run here

Motor Wiring Harness Connection

Suspension Rods

Suspension Dampers

Tub Drain Hose

Drive Motor   Clutch   Drain Pump

The fill valve is accessible on the left. Unlike water valves of the past, the fill strainer screens are plastic and removable. They have a little tab in the middle that you can grab with a pair of needlenose pliers to remove and clean or replace them.

Inside the console, there is also a "mini-manual" containing condensed disassembly instructions and a wiring diagram.

Unlike switchblocks of the past, the selector switches and water level switch are not held in place by screws. There is a locking tab on each. (Figure FA-4) You pry up the tab with the screwdriver and twist it counterclockwise to remove it. Installation is just the opposite; put the switch in place and twist it clockwise until the locking tab clicks.

Unlike the other switches in the panel, timers are held in place by one screw. The timer dial is held to the shaft by a clip. To remove it, pull it until the timer clicks into the "run" position, then reach

Figure FA-4: Console Switch Removal

To remove switches:

Pry up tab and twist switch counterclockwise

behind it with a flat screwdriver and poke the clip off. To re-install it, put the clip on the back of the dial, then line it up and push it onto the timer shaft.

Unlike the old clamshell timers of the past, these timers are throw-away items; they are not rebuildable. They are also impulse-step timers: you sometimes have to wait two or three minutes for something to happen, unlike the old sequence timers, where you could literally watch them clicking off time.

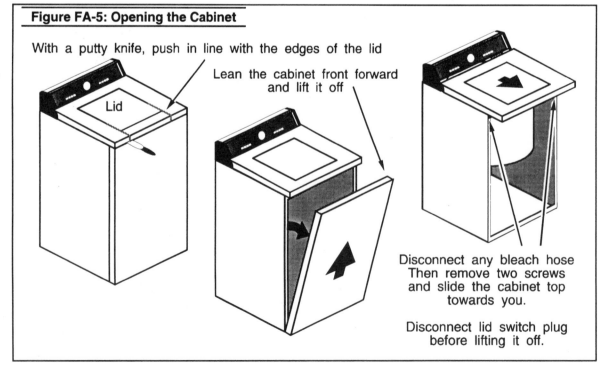

Figure FA-5: Opening the Cabinet

With a putty knife, push in line with the edges of the lid

Lid

Lean the cabinet front forward and lift it off

Disconnect any bleach hose Then remove two screws and slide the cabinet top towards you.

Disconnect lid switch plug before lifting it off.

6-4 CABINET FRONT ACCESS

To access the pump, belt, clutch or drive motor, you need to remove the front panel. The front panel of these machines is held in place by two spring catches at the top, and rests on two tabs at the bottom. Remove as shown in figure FA-5.

Removal of either the drive motor or pump is pretty straightforward. To remove the belt, loosen the motor mounting bolts to relieve belt tension. In certain positions, the transmission may block the drive motor from coming out. If so, physically turn the transmission until there is clearance.

The whole clutch comes off in one piece as shown in figure FA-6 and is replaced as a unit. The clip that holds the clutch on must be bent to remove it and is not reuseable. Replace.

A short word about the suspension. The two cylinders at the end of the suspension rods are suspension dampers. They contain springs, but they also seal and compress air, much like an air shock on a car. They are color-coded; the front ones are heavier than the back ones, because of the added weight of the motor and clutch.

6-5 TUB REMOVAL

Drain the tub (as described in chapter 1.)

To replace the lower bearing or transmission, the tub must be removed.

To replace the waterseal, GE says that it is designed with tabs on it, to enable you to remove it with a pair of pliers, *without removing the tranny.* When I tried it, The tabs were not beefy enough and my pliers kept slipping off them. Without the tranny there, the seal popped off easily with the handle of a pair of pliers. If you need to replace the water seal, take out the basket, try it and decide for yourself.

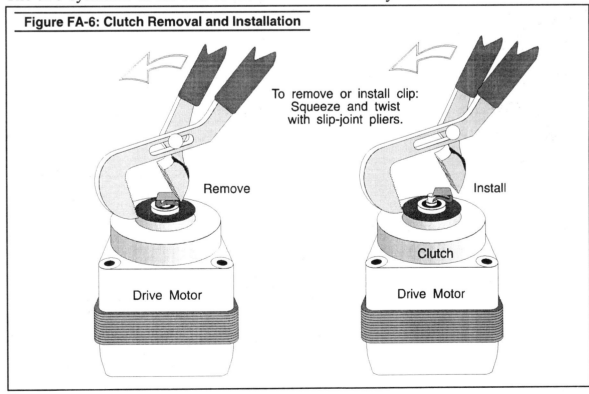

Figure FA-6: Clutch Removal and Installation

To remove or install clip: Squeeze and twist with slip-joint pliers.

Remove

Install

Clutch

Drive Motor

Drive Motor

To remove the tub, first remove the control console as described in section 6-5.

Remove the cabinet front as described in section 6-4.

Remove the cabinet top by removing the screws in the two front corners. The back of the top panel is held on by hooks, so slide it forward and lift it off. Before you remove it completely, disconnect the lid switch wiring harness plug on the right (orange wire & white wire.) Also remove the bleach tube from the front of the cabinet top.

Disconnect the water fill valve and the wiring to it. Remove the 5 screws holding on the backsplash and lift it off; the fill valve will come with it. Remove the screws from the dampening straps (four rubber straps at the top of the tub.)

If you are going to be removing the transmission, remove the agitator and basket. If you are just servicing the lower bearing, skip the next three steps. You do not need to remove the basket, although the tub will be heavier when you remove it with the basket in it)

Remove the agitator by slipping a belt underneath it as shown in figure FA-7, and tugging upwards sharply.

Caution: The agitator comes flying outta there pretty fast, and it can hit you in the face if you're not careful.

Remove the bolt and the plastic air bell. Note that besides holding the agitator, the air bell contains air to keep water away from the transmission oil seal. So the O-ring on the bolt that holds the air bell in place is an important air seal and must be in good shape. (figure FA-7)

The basket can be removed by removing the basket nut under the air bell. Note that this is an aluminum, left-handed nut (turn clockwise to unscrew). They are on VERY tight and being aluminum, they are easy to damage. There is a special slugging spanner wrench to remove these nuts; unfortunately, they're not cheap. However, do not use an open end wrench; you WILL damage the nut. Do not heat it either... it is WAY too close to the transmission oil seal.

At this point you can remove the tub crown if you just need to get under the basket. If you're removing the tub, wait till it's out to remove the tub crown & basket. It's a little easier.

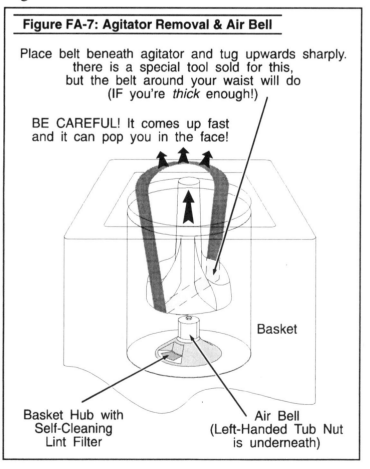

Figure FA-7: Agitator Removal & Air Bell

Place belt beneath agitator and tug upwards sharply. there is a special tool sold for this, but the belt around your waist will do (IF you're *thick* enough!)

BE CAREFUL! It comes up fast and it can pop you in the face!

Basket

Basket Hub with Self-Cleaning Lint Filter

Air Bell (Left-Handed Tub Nut is underneath)

Down below in the tub area, disconnect the pressure switch tube from left side of the tub, and bleach hose if installed. Disconnect the tub drain hose at the tub end.

Unplug the wiring harness(es) from motor and unwind from the right suspension rod.

Lift the front of the tub off the suspension rods and snap the brackets out of the motor platform.

Tilt the transmission forward and disengage rear suspension. Careful, it's heavy. Then tilt the tub either forward or backwards to remove it from the cabinet.

Pop off the eight clips holding on the tub crown. Note that three sides of the crown have forks that fit over knobs on the side of the tub, so it can only go on one way.)

Remove the basket and the split ring and washer underneath it from the top of the transmission casing. When re-installing, note that the tapered side of the split ring goes upward.

Flip the tub assembly upside down and set it on the ground.

Squeeze the belt with your hand and remove the pulley bolt and the pulley. Note that the ribs on the pulley stick upwards.

The lower bearing assembly is now accessible. A rebuild kit is available for (at the time of this writing) about $75, with the special tools necessary available for about $50 more. See section 6-6 to rebuild.

To remove the transmission, cut the cable tie holding the overflow pipe to the motor platform. Remove the four bolts holding the motor platform to the transmission, and the four bolts holding the platform to the tub. Remove the motor platform and pull the transmission straight out. There is a washer (shim) between the transmission and the tub. The transmission and brake are one unit and are replaced together. The transmission is a throw-away item and is not rebuildable.

The tub bearing is not replaceable; if it is bad you must replace the tub. The water seal is replaceable. Using the handles of a pair of pliers, pop it out from the inside of the tub and press a new one in by hand.

6-6 REBUILDING THE LOWER BEARING (Figure FA-8)

There is a bearing kit to replace the lower bearing. Virtually all the parts shown are thrown away and replaced. There is an adjustment to be made in installing the new bearing. Several different pulley hubs are included in the bearing kit; each is a different thickness. There are metal guages and instructions also included in the bearing kit.

There's also a set of special tools to change it out. They're expensive, but the hub tool (part of the kit) is necessary to make the final adjustment.

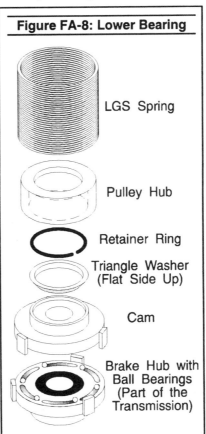

Figure FA-8: Lower Bearing

LGS Spring

Pulley Hub

Retainer Ring

Triangle Washer (Flat Side Up)

Cam

Brake Hub with Ball Bearings (Part of the Transmission)

Chapter 7

MAYTAG

(Performa models, see Norge - Chapter 9)

7-1 BASIC OPERATION

The design uses a reversing motor, which is belted to both the pump and the transmission, using two different belts. At times, both one-speed and two-speed motors were used. When viewed from the top, the motor turns clockwise for the agitation cycle, and counterclockwise for the spin cycle. (Figure M-1)

To switch between the two cycles, there is a brake in the hub of the drive pulley, and a clutch in the transmission.

During agitation, the brake keeps the transmission casing from turning, and the drive pulley turns the transmission shaft. During the spin cycle, the brake releases and the whole transmission starts slowly spinning around. Since the basket is attached to the transmission casing, it spins, too. A clutch built into the transmission allows slippage until the basket gets up to speed. At the end of the spin cycle, the motor stops and the brake brings the basket to a stop.

In the late '80's, Maytag redesigned the transmission. The result is the "orbital" transmission, which has just a few moving parts and is serviceable in the machine. One is supposed to be able to replace the other directly. However, the gearing in the orbital is higher (the agitator agitates faster) so I would not replace one with the other unless absolutely unavoidable; for example, if the parts were unavailable.

The motor is mounted on rollers which ride in a metal track. Springs attached to the motor mounting plate keep tension on the belts.

The pump reverses with the motor, but there is no recirculation. When the washer is agitating, the pump is just sitting there spinning; it is not moving any water.

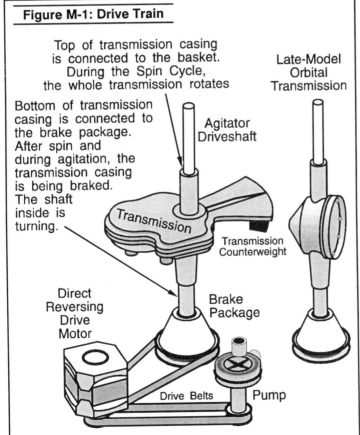

Figure M-1: Drive Train

Top of transmission casing is connected to the basket. During the Spin Cycle, the whole transmission rotates

Bottom of transmission casing is connected to the brake package. After spin and during agitation, the transmission casing is being braked. The shaft inside is turning.

Late-Model Orbital Transmission

Agitator Driveshaft

Transmission

Transmission Counterweight

Direct Reversing Drive Motor

Brake Package

Drive Belts   Pump

7-2 OPENING THE CABINET AND CONSOLE

To access the belts, lean the machine against the wall and look underneath. Follow the safety precautions described in section 1-5(3).

To open the front of the cabinet, remove the two screws at the bottom of the front panel. (Figure M-2.) Raise the panel fairly high and the top clips will disengage from the cabinet top.

To raise the cabinet top, remove the two screws on the underside of the front corners.

Two types of consoles were used in different machines. To open the console, see figure M-2.

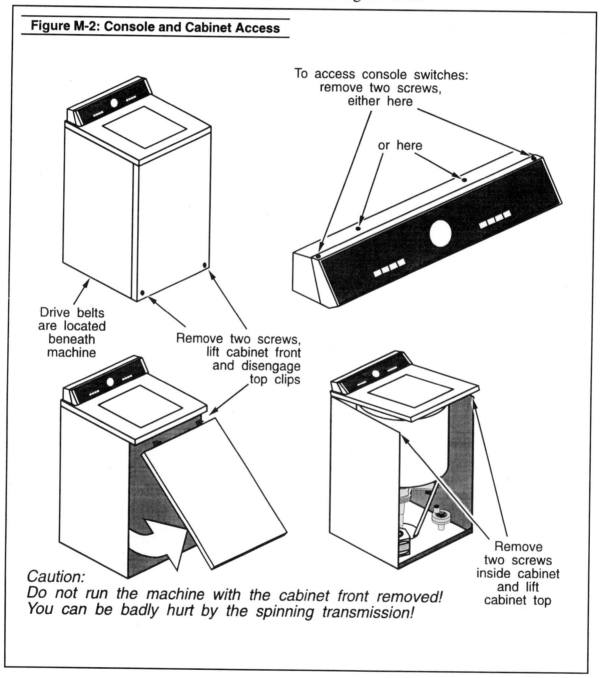

Figure M-2: Console and Cabinet Access

To access console switches:
remove two screws,
either here

or here

Drive belts are located beneath machine

Remove two screws, lift cabinet front and disengage top clips

Remove two screws inside cabinet and lift cabinet top

Caution:
Do not run the machine with the cabinet front removed! You can be badly hurt by the spinning transmission!

7-3 DIAGNOSIS

The lid switch plunger is located in the center rear of the lid. With the lid up, NOTHING on these machines works. In order to diagnose these machines, you need to keep the lid up far enough to look inside, without tripping the lid switch. You can do this by inserting a putty knife between the lid and the switch, and then propping up the lid with something (I use my electrical pliers to prop up the lid.)

The most common ailments in a Maytag washer are leaks, worn belts, and broken timers.

DIAGNOSIS 1: WATER LEAKS

Besides the usual leaky fill solenoid valves, bleach dispensers and such (section 2-6) there are many places that a Maytag washer commonly leaks.

1) In the fill line, between the fill solenoid valve and the tub fill nozzle, there is a fill injector which prevents any accidental siphoning of wash water back into your house's fresh water system. (Figure M-3.) This fill injector can get clogged with calcium or other deposits, causing it to back up and leak. It is easily replaced. It is located beneath the cabinet top, on the left side.

2) If you have a large leak from inside the right rear of the machine, it is probably coming from the drain hose anti-siphon valve. (See figure G-7 in chapter 2.) This is the valve in the washer drain line, right where it penetrates the rear of the cabinet. This valve is easily replaced.

NOTE: Not all models were equipped with this valve.

3) The tub seal will leak from the center of the tub, directly onto the top of the transmission. A tub stem & seal kit is available from your appliance parts dealer. See section 7-12.

4) Sometimes, tub hoses or fittings will leak. There are soft lead washers that seal the tub braces, where the bolts enter the tub. You must remove the basket to replace these lead washers; see section 7-12.

5) The pump can leak; see section 7-4.

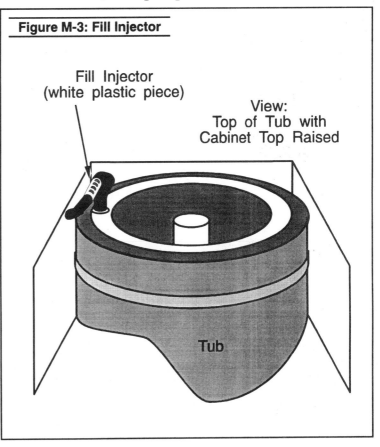

Figure M-3: Fill Injector

Fill Injector (white plastic piece)

View: Top of Tub with Cabinet Top Raised

Tub

DIAGNOSIS 2: BASKET SPINS, BUT WATER DOESN'T PUMP OUT

Check for a broken or worn pump belt. Replace as described in section 7-10.

With the machine in "spin," look at the pump pulley beneath the machine with a mirror. If it is spinning, but water is not pumping, check for a clog in the hose between the tub and pump. If there is no jam, replace the pump as described in section 7-4.

If the pump is not turning, see section 7-4.

DIAGNOSIS 3: WASHER FILLS, BUT DOESN'T AGITATE AND/OR SPIN

1) Check the imbalance/lid switch (Section 7-6) for continuity. Check also the speed selector switch (if any), the water level and water temperature switches for proper operation as described in section 2-5.

NOTE: If any of the selector switches on the console are only partially pushed in, it may cause improper function.

2) Check for a broken or badly worn belt. (Section 7-10)

3) Check the motor rollers and tension springs for damage and the motor roller tracks for jamming. (Section 7-10) Any of these might cause the belt to be loose.

4) Check the appropriate timer circuits for continuity. (See section 2-5(c).

5) Remove the belts and see if the motor will start. If you hear the motor buzzing, but it doesn't start in either or both directions, test the capacitor (if any) and starting switch as described in sections 2-5(e) and 7-8. If it does start with the load removed, turn the pump and transmission pulleys by hand, in both directions, to see which is locked up. If the pump is locked, see section 7-4. If the transmission pulley is locked, see section 7-9. Note that the transmission pulley will normally be very stiff when turning it in the clockwise direction, as you look at the bottom of the washer.

6) If the washer spins but does not agitate, check the agitator splines as described in section 7-11. If they are not the problem, the transmission needs to be replaced; see section 7-9.

DIAGNOSIS 4: BASKET SPINS (CCW) WHILE AGITATING

Replace the brake package as described in section 7-13.

DIAGNOSIS 5: NOISY OPERATION OR EXCESSIVE VIBRATION

If both motor springs break, the motor shaft will touch the baseplate of the machine, causing an enormous racket. (See section 7-10.)

If the machine squeaks or vibrates too much in spin (and redistributing the clothes doesn't seem to help) check the damper pads as described in section 7-14.

If you are getting a short screeching noise during braking (at the very end of the spin cycle,) the brake needs to be lubricated. See section 7-13.

7-4 PUMP AND PUMP BELT

Remove the pump belt and check to see if the pump will turn freely by hand. If not, check for a jam as described in section 2-3. Probe around the inside of the hoses or pump with needlenose pliers. If the pump won't turn easily, and you can't find anything jamming it, replace the pump. The bearings are bad.

If the pump turns freely by hand, but the belt doesn't drive it, see section 7-10.

Belt adjustment on a Maytag is relatively loose. Pinch the pump belt together with your fingers at the center. If you have more than a 1/4" gap, the belt is too tight. (Figure M-4.) Loosen the pump mounts to adjust.

Figure M-4: Belt Adjustment

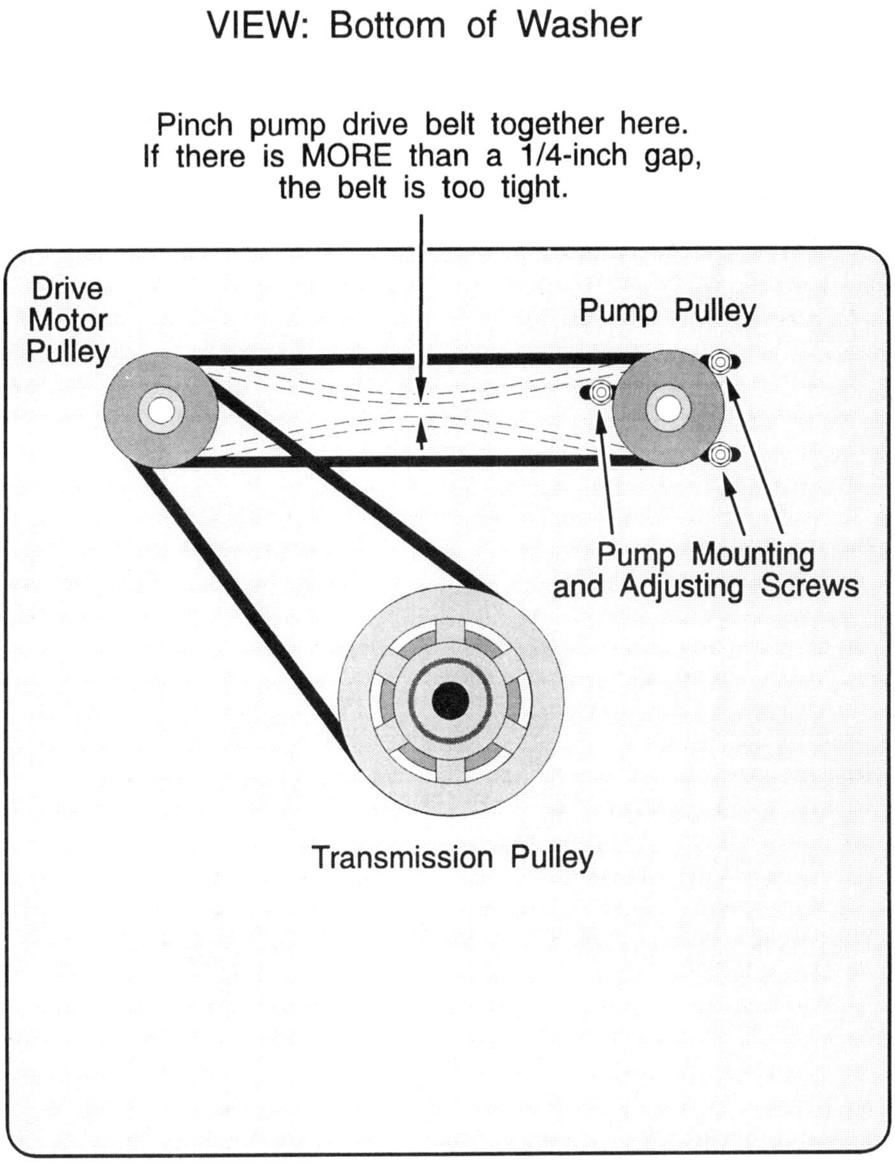

VIEW: Bottom of Washer

Pinch pump drive belt together here.
If there is MORE than a 1/4-inch gap,
the belt is too tight.

Drive Motor Pulley

Pump Pulley

Pump Mounting and Adjusting Screws

Transmission Pulley

7-5 WATER LEVEL SWITCH

Refer to section 2-5 (b) and compare with figure M-5 to test the switch for proper operation. Replace if defective.

7-6 IMBALANCE/LID SWITCH

The lid switch on these machines is located inside the control console. The mechanical linkage that activates it can be found by lifting the cabinet top. (See Figure M-6)

Installation of a new lid switch involves an adjustment. Some models have an adjustment screw as shown in Figure M-6. On other models, adjustment is made by loosening the switch mounting screws. The lid switch should open when the lid is raised 1 to 2 inches.

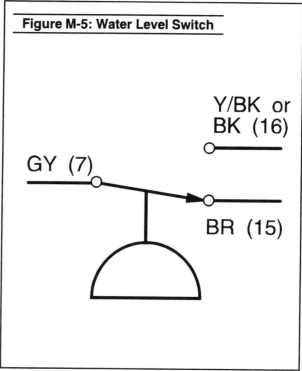

Figure M-5: Water Level Switch

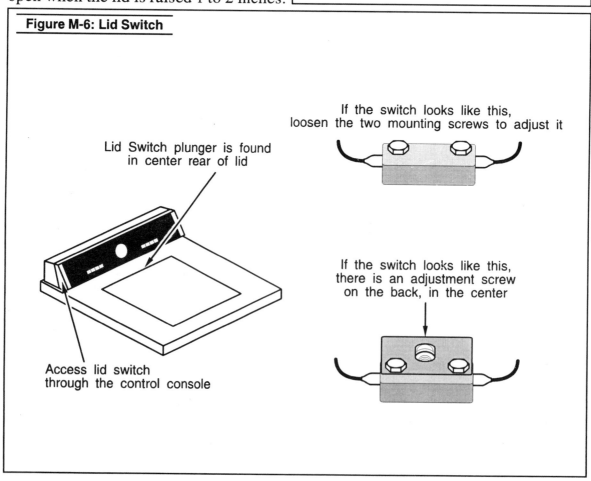

Figure M-6: Lid Switch

Lid Switch plunger is found in center rear of lid

Access lid switch through the control console

If the switch looks like this, loosen the two mounting screws to adjust it

If the switch looks like this, there is an adjustment screw on the back, in the center

7-7 TIMER

The motor in Maytag timers can be removed and replaced separately from the timer body itself. If the timer is not advancing properly, you can try replacing just the motor.

To access the timer for testing, remove the console panel as described in section 7-2.

To remove the timer, pry the cap off the knob (Figure M-7.) Using a pair of needlenose pliers, remove the spring clip that holds the timer knob in place. Remove the knob, spring and dial. Beneath the dial are the two timer mounting screws.

To remove the timer motor from the timer body, simply remove the two motor mounting screws and the two motor terminals.

7-8 DRIVE MOTOR AND STARTING SWITCH

Some machines may have external capacitors. Test as described in section 2-5(e).

Maytag motors have a piggyback centrifugal starting switch. Compared to other brands, they are very complex motors. They are not only direct-reversing, but some are multi-speed, too. Unfortunately, just about every model had the starting switch wired differently. To make matters worse, the motor wire colors do not always correspond with the colors marked on the switch. Whenever removing the motor or switch from the machine, mark which wires came off which of the switch terminals. Draw a picture if you must. Make sure you dif-

Figure M-7: Timer Dial Removal

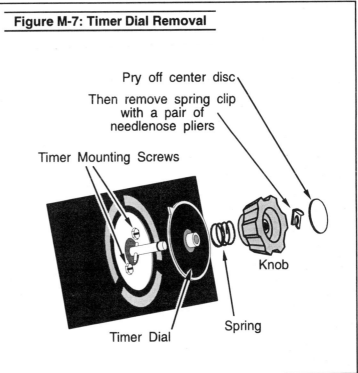

ferentiate in your notes between a motor wire and a wiring harness wire of the same color, and where each goes on the switch.

If the drive motor does not start, try replacing the starting switch as described in section 2-5(e). Make sure you get the right switch for your machine. If the motor STILL doesn't start, replace it.

To remove the motor, first remove power from the machine. Remove the plastic water shield from the motor, and mark and remove the wires.

Remove the drive belts. Remove the motor pulley from the motor shaft. Remove the four motor baseplate screws and lift the motor and baseplate out of the machine.

Installation is the opposite of removal. Sometimes a replacement motor is wired differently than the original. Make sure you check the box that the new motor comes in for a wiring diagram.

7-9 TRANSMISSION

I do not recommend the novice trying to replace a transmission in a Maytag washer. If the transmission drive pulley is locked up, call a qualified service technician or junk the washer.

7-10 MOTOR ROLLERS, TENSION SPRINGS AND BELTS

Disconnect power and remove the front panel of your washer.

The drive motor is mounted on rollers, and belt tension is kept by two springs. (Figure M-8)

If one of these springs breaks, there may not be enough belt tension to drive the transmission and/or pump. If both break, there will be NO tension on the belts and in addition, the motor shaft will probably be hitting the washer baseplate, causing a heck of a racket.

The roller tracks can get clogged up with dirt, soap deposits or other obstructions. If so, clean out the tracks so the motor rolls freely. Lubricate the rollers and tracks with a little wheel bearing grease.

Examine the condition of each belt as described in section 2-4(a). Always replace BOTH belts if one is bad. Never replace just one belt.

To replace, simply push the motor towards the transmission pulley and slip the belts off.

Only the pump belt needs to have the proper tension set. Pump belt tension is explained in section 7-4.

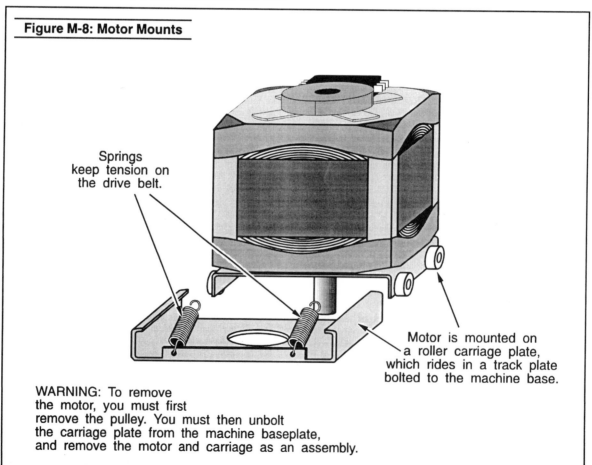

Figure M-8: Motor Mounts

Springs keep tension on the drive belt.

Motor is mounted on a roller carriage plate, which rides in a track plate bolted to the machine base.

WARNING: To remove the motor, you must first remove the pulley. You must then unbolt the carriage plate from the machine baseplate, and remove the motor and carriage as an assembly.

7-11 AGITATOR SPLINES

Most Maytag washers have an agitator that lifts directly out. These models have a rubber stop ring around the agitator shaft at the bottom of the splines. The agitator feels like it "snaps" onto the shaft.

A few models had a set screw that must be loosened before removing the agitator.

If the washer is not agitating, remove the agitator. Look at the splines and the agitator shaft. If the shaft is agitating, and the plastic splines in the agitator look stripped, replace the agitator.

When replacing the agitator, be sure you push it down until you feel it snap over the rubber stop ring at the bottom of the agitator splines.

7-12 TUB, BASKET, STEM & SEAL

To remove the basket, first remove the agitator as described in section 7-11.

Remove the clamp holding the tub

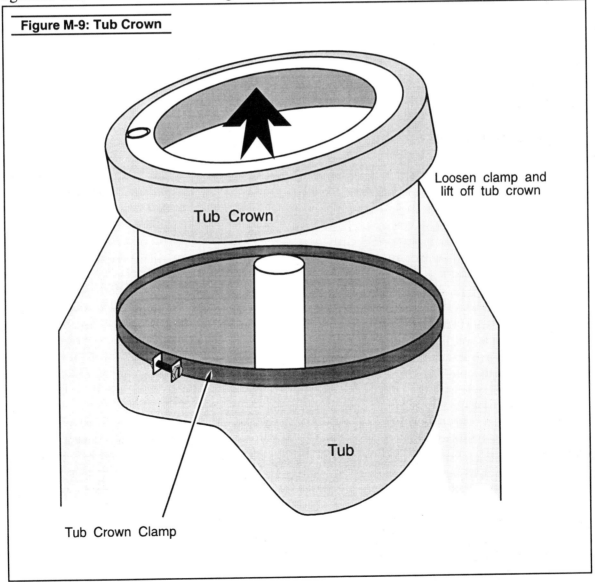

Figure M-9: Tub Crown

Loosen clamp and lift off tub crown

Tub Crown

Tub

Tub Crown Clamp

crown to the tub. Remove the tub crown. (Figure M-9)

To remove the spanner nut holding the basket down, you must get a special spanner wrench (it's available from your parts dealer, and not too expensive.) Remove the spanner nut and the washer beneath it. (Figure M-10.) Tap with a rubber or plastic mallet to remove.

CAUTION: This spanner nut has a LEFTHAND thread; you must turn the nut CLOCKWISE to remove it.

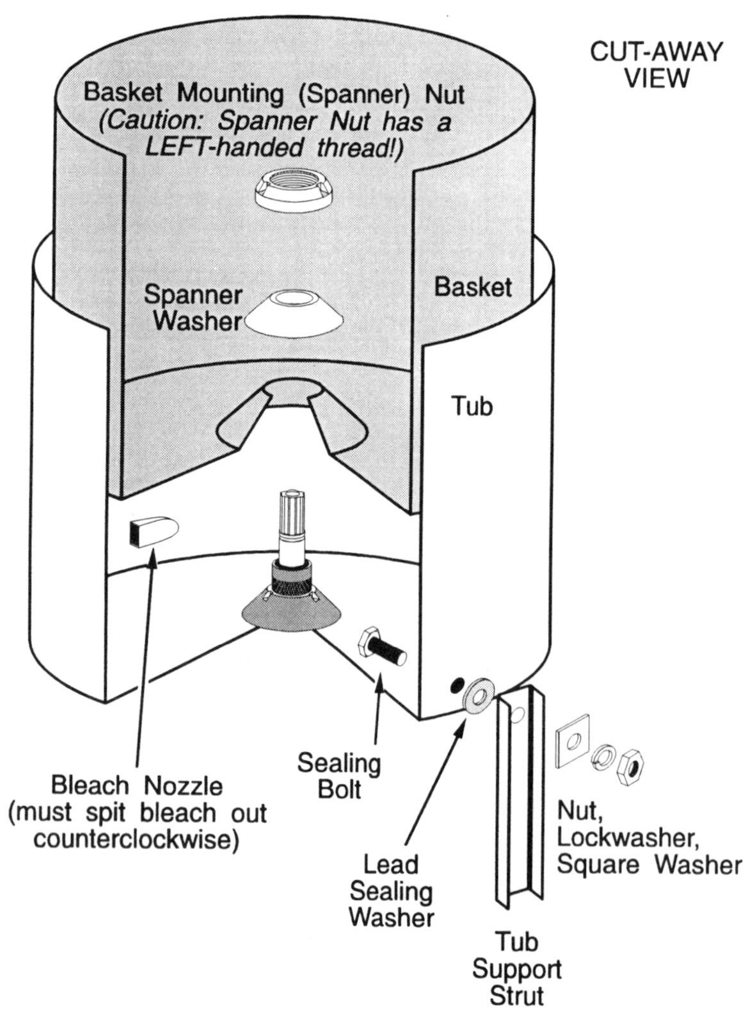

Lift out the basket.

If you need to replace a leaking bleach deflector nozzle, (Figure M-10) pull the tab off the outside of the nozzle and snap it out of the tub. To replace, make sure the nozzle spits out bleach in a counterclockwise direction. (Figure M-10)

There are soft lead washers that seal the tub mounting bolts where the damper struts mount to the tub.)(Figure M-10) If they are leaking, replace them by removing the tub mounting bolts one at a time. Make sure you put the soft lead washer between the tub and the strut. The square washer, lock washer and nut go on the outside of the strut. When you tighten, make sure you tighten the *nut* and hold the *bolt*. If you turn the bolt to tighten, it will break the seal between the soft lead washer and the bolt, and the machine will continue leaking.

TUB BOOT SEAL

If the tub boot is leaking, get a stem & seal kit from your appliance parts dealer.

To replace the boot seal and center shaft seal, remove the rubber stop ring at the base of the agitator shaft splines (Figure M-11.) With a screwdriver, pry out the retaining washer lock ring, the retaining washer and the center shaft seal from around the center shaft.

Figure M-10: Basket Removal and Tub Fittings

CUT-AWAY VIEW

Basket Mounting (Spanner) Nut *(Caution: Spanner Nut has a LEFT-handed thread!)*

Spanner Washer

Basket

Tub

Bleach Nozzle (must spit bleach out counterclockwise)

Sealing Bolt

Lead Sealing Washer

Nut, Lockwasher, Square Washer

Tub Support Strut

With an allen head wrench, loosen the set screw in the tub mounting stem. (Figure M-11.) Using the same spanner wrench you used to remove the tub, remove the tub mounting stem.

CAUTION: The tub mounting stem has a LEFTHAND thread; turn the stem CLOCKWISE to remove it.

Remove the old boot seal by turning it as you pull up on the bottom of it.

To reassemble, wet the inside of the bottom lip of the seal with a little bit of spit and twist it down onto the tub lip to seat it evenly. DO NOT push on the carbon ring to seat the seal on the tub lip; in fact, try not to touch the carbon ring any more than is absolutely necessary.

Tighten the tub mounting stem by hand, (remember; left hand thread, so turn CCW to tighten.) Put the special spanner wrench on it and tap it with a mallet to tighten it.

To install the set screw, tighten it hard to dimple the transmission casing, then back off the set screw and tighten it firmly (but not very hard.)

NOTE: There should be 2 to 4 threads showing on the set screw. If NO threads are showing, remove the set screw and tighten the tub mounting stem another 1/8 of a turn, then re-install the set screw.

The rest of installation is the opposite of removal. Don't forget the left-hand thread on the spanner nut; tighten by turning it CCW.

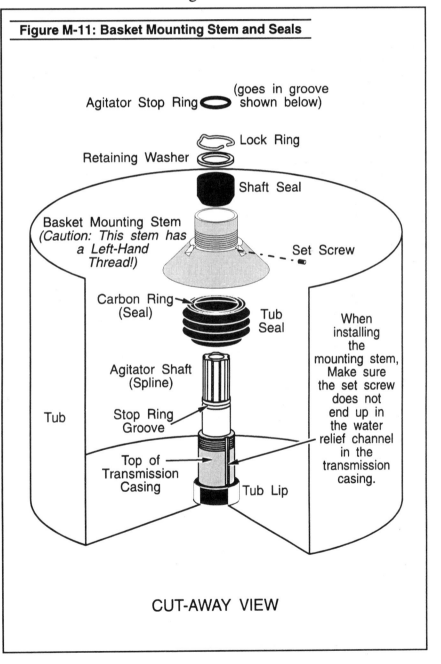

Figure M-11: Basket Mounting Stem and Seals

Agitator Stop Ring — (goes in groove shown below)

Lock Ring

Retaining Washer

Shaft Seal

Basket Mounting Stem *(Caution: This stem has a Left-Hand Thread!)*

Set Screw

Carbon Ring (Seal)

Tub Seal

When installing the mounting stem, Make sure the set screw does not end up in the water relief channel in the transmission casing.

Agitator Shaft (Spline)

Tub

Stop Ring Groove

Top of Transmission Casing

Tub Lip

CUT-AWAY VIEW

7-13 BRAKE PACKAGE

Remove power from the machine and remove the front panel. Pad the floor to prevent scratching the cabinet, and lay the machine on its back. Block up the tub so the tub remains in line with the cabinet.

Beneath the washer, in the center, is the brake package. The brake package changes the machine from the spin to the drain cycle and back when the motor reverses. It also brakes the spinning basket at the end of the spin cycle or when the lid is lifted.

The brake lining is normally lubricated by a few drops of oil. If the lining gets too dry, it can start squeaking at the very end of the spin cycle, when it is braking the basket. Lubricate by squirting in two or three shots of 40-weight oil (from a regular pump-type oiler) as shown in Figure M-12.

The brake package is not too expensive and can be replaced if defective.

Replacement requires a special tool which is not too expensive either. You can remove and replace the brake package, but *DO NOT DISASSEMBLE THE PACKAGE YOURSELF. IT IS HEAVILY SPRING LOADED. YOU MAY HURT YOURSELF OPENING IT, AND IT IS IMPRACTICAL FOR YOU TO TRY TO REBUILD IT YOURSELF.*

BRAKE PACKAGE REMOVAL

Remove the center screw from the driveshaft. Remove the drive lug from the splines on the shaft. Remove the drive pulley by turning counterclockwise (as you look at the bottom of the washer.) Remove the bolt and retainer clip shown in figure M-13.

Using the special spanner tool, unscrew the brake package from the washer base by tapping with a mallet. When it is unscrewed from the baseplate, pull the package straight off to disengage it from the splines on the bottom of the transmission casing.

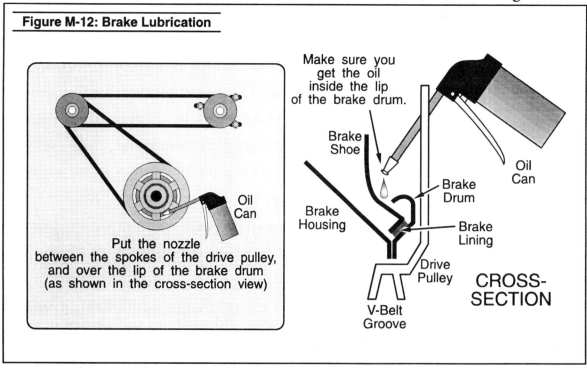

Figure M-12: Brake Lubrication

Put the nozzle between the spokes of the drive pulley, and over the lip of the brake drum (as shown in the cross-section view)

Make sure you get the oil inside the lip of the brake drum.

Brake Shoe

Brake Housing

Brake Drum

Brake Lining

Oil Can

Drive Pulley

V-Belt Groove

CROSS-SECTION

BRAKE PACKAGE INSTALLATION

When installing the brake package, it is important to have the transmission shaft parallel to the cabinet. This will help you to thread the brake package into the base plate without cross-threading it. With the tub blocked up, grab the bottom of the transmission casing and move it by hand until you can slip the brake package onto the splines. Turn the transmission casing and the brake package together. If you don't, you will be trying to overcome brake pressure to turn the

package. Turn the transmission and brake package until the brake package is hand tight in the baseplate. Then tighten firmly with the special spanner tool and a hammer or mallet. Install the bolt and retaining clip.

Place the pulley bearing on the driveshaft with the cupped side towards the pulley. Install the drive pulley on the helical shaft. While holding the transmission so it doesn't turn, run the drive pulley up as tight as you can by hand onto the helical shaft.

Figure M-13: Brake Package Removal

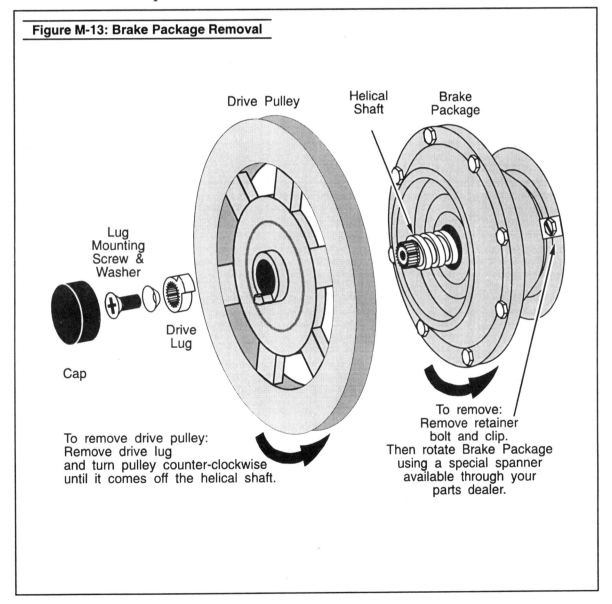

Cap

Lug Mounting Screw & Washer

Drive Lug

Drive Pulley

Helical Shaft

Brake Package

To remove drive pulley:
Remove drive lug and turn pulley counter-clockwise until it comes off the helical shaft.

To remove:
Remove retainer bolt and clip. Then rotate Brake Package using a special spanner available through your parts dealer.

You will see a drive lug on the pulley that corresponds to the shaft drive lug. (Figure M-14) With the flat side of the shaft drive lug towards the pulley, install the shaft drive lug on the shaft splines so that the lug is 180 degrees from the pulley drive lug.

Hold the transmission and turn the pulley gently counterclockwise to release tension from the brake spring. Keep turning the pulley until the two drive lugs just touch. Then turn the pulley gently clockwise until you just barely begin to feel the brake spring pressure. The shaft lug should be at about 9 o'clock from the pulley lug. If not, adjust the shaft lug on the splines.

The idea is to get the pulley to bottom out on the helical drive shaft just as the drive lugs touch. Sometimes it takes two or three tries to get this adjustment correct. If it is not correct, you will hear the drive motor bogging down and perhaps tripping on the overload during the agitation cycle.

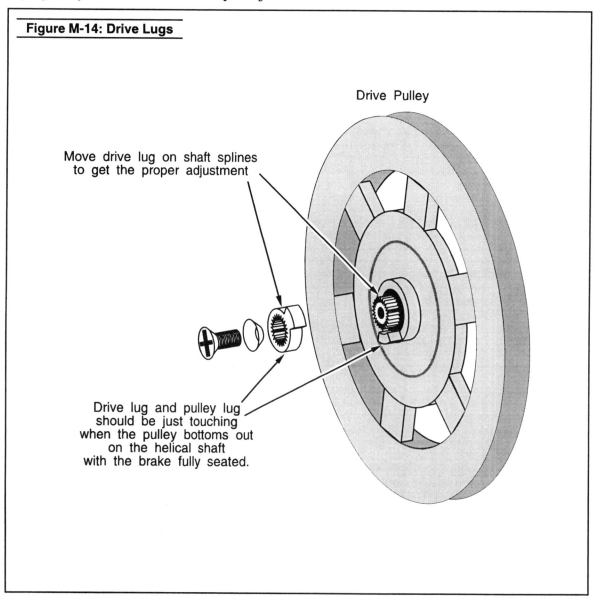

Figure M-14: Drive Lugs

Drive Pulley

Move drive lug on shaft splines to get the proper adjustment

Drive lug and pulley lug should be just touching when the pulley bottoms out on the helical shaft with the brake fully seated.

7-14 DAMPER PADS

The damper supports the weight of the water in the tub. It is also the pivot of an imbalanced tub. (Figure M-15)

Beneath the damper plate are damper pads, which provide the friction and wear surface. They can wear out, causing metal-to-metal contact and squeaking.

Reach under the washer and remove the drive belt.

Remove the cabinet front and tilt up the cabinet top. Mark the position of the nuts on the three eyebolts (Figure M-15) and remove the bottom nuts. This will remove spring tension on the tub centering springs.

Figure M-15: Damper and Balancing Springs

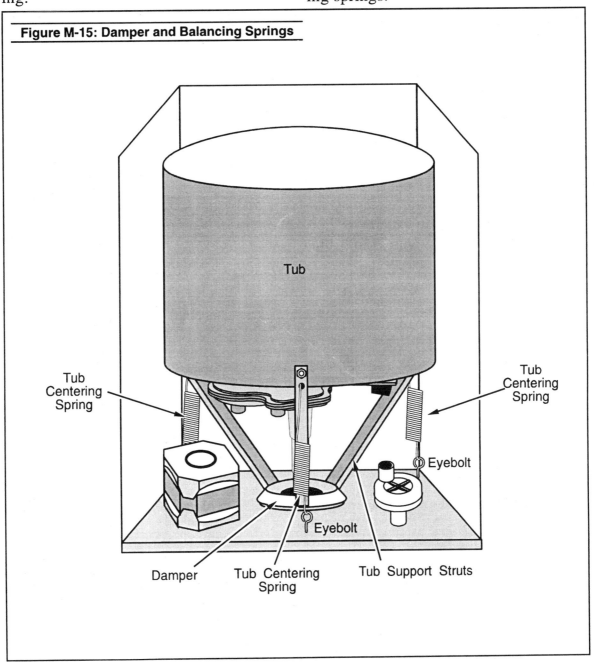

Tub

Tub Centering Spring

Tub Centering Spring

Eyebolt

Eyebolt

Damper

Tub Centering Spring

Tub Support Struts

Lean the washer back against the wall at an angle. Place a 4x4 wood block directly underneath the transmission pulley and lower the machine onto the wood block. This will lift the tub, transmission and damper assembly several inches. (Figure M-16)

If the old damper pads are just dry and not too worn, lubricate them with a sili-cone-based grease, available from your appliance parts dealer.

If the old damper pads look too worn, scrape them off and replace them. Get a damper pad kit from your appliance parts dealer. It should include the glue you need. Use rubbing alcohol to clean and prepare the surface to be glued.

Figure M-16: Replacing the Damper Pads

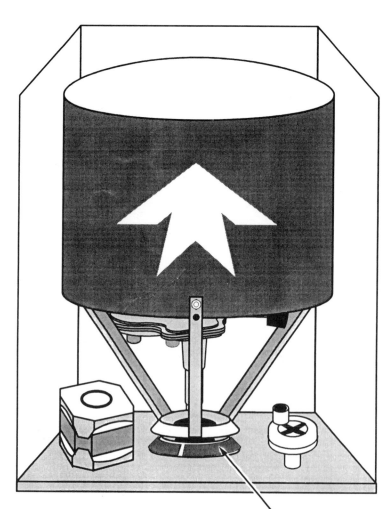

Lift the Tub, Transmission and Damper Assembly by placing a block of wood beneath the brake package and setting the washer down on it

If they are worn out, replace the damper pads by scraping off the old ones and glueing on new pads.

Chapter 8

FLUID-DRIVE (Pre-1980)
SPEED QUEEN / AMANA

Speed Queen has undergone several major design changes in the past few years. There are still significant numbers of all different designs out there, and they are generally not too expensive to repair, so all are included in this manual. In this book, they will be referred to as early model, middle model and late model machines.

Your first duty is to figure out which machine you have. Once you open the cabinet, the most obvious differences are:

1) Early model machines have a fluid drive unit and two solenoids; one at the agitator dogs and one at the fluid drive. They also have three belts.

2) Middle model machines have a fluid drive unit, but no solenoids to engage the spin and agitate cycles. They also have three belts.

3) Late model machines have no fluid drive unit, and only one or two belts. These machines are covered in Chapter 8a.

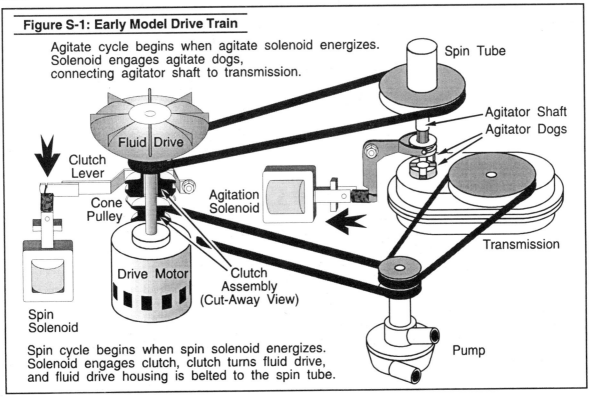

Figure S-1: Early Model Drive Train

Agitate cycle begins when agitate solenoid energizes. Solenoid engages agitate dogs, connecting agitator shaft to transmission.

Spin Tube

Agitator Shaft
Agitator Dogs

Clutch Lever

Fluid Drive

Cone Pulley

Agitation Solenoid

Transmission

Drive Motor

Clutch Assembly (Cut-Away View)

Spin Solenoid

Pump

Spin cycle begins when spin solenoid energizes. Solenoid engages clutch, clutch turns fluid drive, and fluid drive housing is belted to the spin tube.

8-1 BASIC OPERATING SYSTEMS

EARLY MODELS

The early models (Figure S-1) had single-direction motors, and three drive belts. The motor turns constantly, and so do the pump and transmission. The fluid drive (and thus the spin tube) turns only when the spin solenoid is engaged. Solenoids engage and disengage the spin and agitate cycles.

A set of dogs is splined to the transmission shaft (but floats on the spline.) When the solenoid energizes, a yoke pulls these dogs down the shaft spline, into the moving dogs on the transmission. The agitator is then connected to the transmission, and moves. When the dogs disengage, the agitator is free to turn with the spinning basket.

During the spin cycle, the spin solenoid connects the fluid drive to the motor via a clutch arrangement. The fluid drive is belted directly to the spin tube. Like a torque converter in a car, it allows slippage between the motor and the basket, bringing the basket up to speed slowly. This "pre-pump" action allows most of the water to be slung out of the basket before it gets up to full spin speed, preventing a heavy load from being thrown on the motor suddenly.

MIDDLE MODELS (Figure S-2)

The middle models use a direct-reversing motor. The drive system is similar to the early models, except that the cycles are not engaged by solenoids. Rather, a helix in the transmission pulley hub causes the pulley to float upwards when the motor turns counterclockwise (when viewed from the top.) This moves a yoke that engages the agitator dogs.

There is also a helix in the spin (center) pulley. During the agitate cycle, this helix engages a brake in the centerpost,

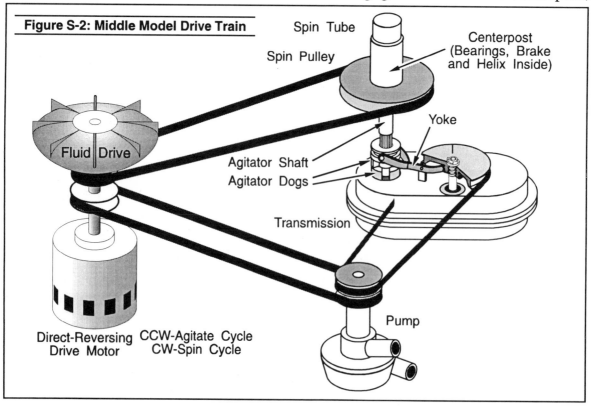

Figure S-2: Middle Model Drive Train

Spin Tube
Spin Pulley
Centerpost (Bearings, Brake and Helix Inside)
Fluid Drive
Yoke
Agitator Shaft
Agitator Dogs
Transmission
Pump
Direct-Reversing Drive Motor
CCW-Agitate Cycle
CW-Spin Cycle

which keeps the basket from turning. During the spin cycle, the brake disengages and the basket is allowed to spin. Belted to the spin pulley is the fluid drive assembly, which is connected directly to the motor shaft. See "EARLY MODELS" above for the function of the fluid drive.

8-2 OPENING THE CABINET AND CONSOLE

The console may be opened as shown in figure S-3.

The cabinet may also be opened as shown in figure S-3; however, the front panel on early models comes off slightly differently. The top of the panel is hooked over a crossbar inside the cabinet. To remove it, lift and pull the panel outwards a little. When the top disengages, drop the whole panel down to remove it.

Figure S-3: Opening the Cabinet and Console

To access console switches: remove four screws, here

and here

Remove screws, lift cabinet front

Remove two screws inside cabinet and lift cabinet top

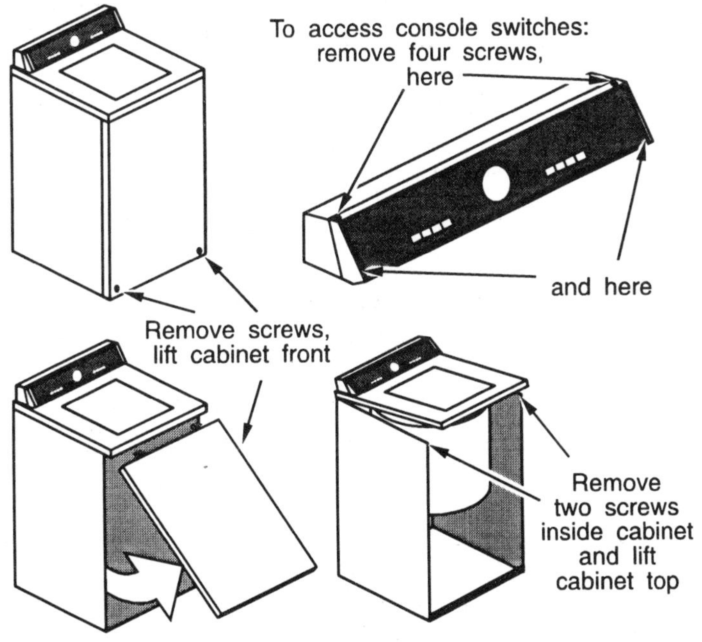

Caution:
Do not run the machine
with the cabinet front removed!
You can be badly hurt by the moving parts inside!

On certain models, the front panel was *hinged* to the top panel.

8-3 DIAGNOSIS

The most common problems with these washers are:

PUMPS

The pump bearings tend to seize after a number of years, causing burned belts, burning rubber smells, no pumping, and other common symptoms. (See Chapter 2, sections 2-3 and 2-4.) To repair or replace, see section 8-4.

BELTS

With three belts on the early and middle models and two on the late models, worn belts are a concern. Symptoms are usual, as described in section 2-3 and 2-4. The late model machines also have a belt tensioner/idler that can seize bearings or break or stretch out springs. Changing belts and servicing the idler is described in section 8-5.

FLUID DRIVE

In early model machines, the center bearing in the fluid drive has been known to seize around the motor shaft, causing the basket to try to spin while the washer in the agitate cycle. In either early OR middle models, the bearings within the drive can also go bad, causing the same symptoms. A bent motor shaft will cause similar symptoms. See section 8-6.

NO AGITATE OR NO SPIN

On early model machines only, the solenoids can burn out or stick. The washer will not enter either the spin cycle or the agitate cycle. (One or the other, but usually not both) See section 8-7.

In both models, a broken belt will cause this symptom. See section 8-5.

In all models, if the washer won't agitate or agitates only weakly, the agitator drive block can be worn. See section 8-9.

LEAKS

The most common leaks in these machines come from hoses, pump seals and tub fittings. There is also a boot seal between the centerpost and the tub that can leak. Basket removal and boot seal replacement is discussed in section 8-10.

In early and middle models, the water may appear to be draining out of the tub as soon as the agitation cycle starts. This symptom is usually accompanied by a clattering noise during the spin cycle. Chances are, the sediment tube is broken off; see section 8-10.

NOISES

A clattering noise during the agitation cycle usually means that the agitator dogs are worn. To replace, see section 8-8.

In early and middle models, you may hear a clattering noise during the spin cycle. This usually means that the sediment tube is broken off; see the *LEAKS* heading above and section 8-10.

8-4 PUMPS (Figure S-4)

Pumps in the early and middle model machines *can* be rebuilt, but I do not recommend it. First, it's not easy. Second, the pot metal parts tend to deteriorate over time, and with exposure to detergents and such. And third, new pumps are cheap enough that it's just not worth the effort.

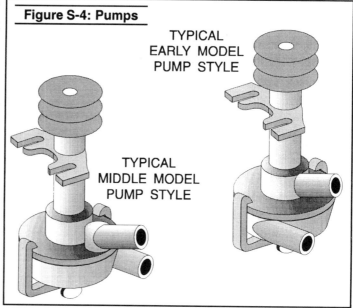

Figure S-4: Pumps

TYPICAL EARLY MODEL PUMP STYLE

TYPICAL MIDDLE MODEL PUMP STYLE

Figure S-5: Belt Adjustment

Cut-Away View from Top of Washer Downward

Transmission Pulley

Spin Pulley

Motor Mounting Plate and Adjustment Bolts

Pump Pulley and Mounting/ Adjusting Bolts

Motor Pulley

Proper Adjustment is 1/2" on all 3 belts

Motor Pivot Bolt

Many different pumps were used in the various models. When you go to your parts dealer, make sure you bring your washer's model number, or the old pump, to make sure you get the right one.

8-5 BELTS

EARLY AND MIDDLE MODELS

There are three belts in the early and middle model washers. Except for the spin belt is tricky, and also the pump belt in early models, but otherwise, replacement is easy. Just loosen the adjustment bolts (Figure S-5) for the belt you're replacing, and slip it off.

To replace the spin belt on both models, remove the agitator dogs as described in section 8-8.

To remove the pump belt in early models, you must get it past the fluid drive. After removing the spin belt, remove the entire motor / fluid drive / spin solenoid assembly as described in section 8-6. Then remove the cam bolt, disconnect the solenoid from the clutch lever (Figure S-6) and lift the fluid drive off the motor shaft. The belt can then be replaced easily. Assembly is the opposite of disassembly. Be sure to adjust the clutch lever as described in section 8-6.

Proper belt tension is when you can deflect the belt about 1/2", midway between each pair of pulleys, with normal finger pressure. To adjust belt tension, loosen all three belts. First adjust the spin belt tension by moving the motor, and secure the motor mount bolts. Then adjust both the pump and transmission belts at the same time, by moving the pump.

8-6 FLUID DRIVE

If the washer is trying to spin and agitate at the same time, there *may* be a problem with your fluid drive, or the motor shaft may be bent. To determine which, you must first remove the motor/ fluid drive assembly from the machine. Loosen the motor mounting plate mounting bolts, and disengage the belts from their respective pullies. Then lift out the assembly.

Hold the motor shaft and try turning the fluid drive housing now.

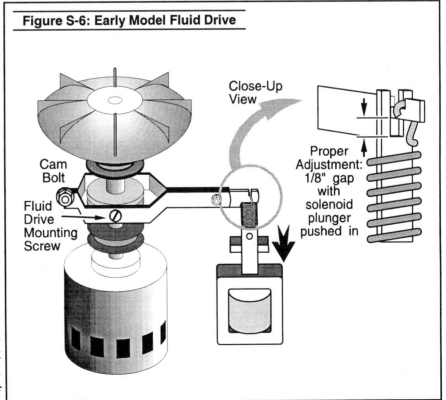

Figure S-6: Early Model Fluid Drive

Cam Bolt

Fluid Drive Mounting Screw

Close-Up View

Proper Adjustment: 1/8" gap with solenoid plunger pushed in

MIDDLE MODELS

If the fluid drive does not turn freely, it is bad. Use a straight punch to punch out the roll pin holding it to the motor shaft and replace it.

CAUTION: When punching the roll pin in or out, you MUST support the motor shaft solidly. You can easily bend it.

EARLY MODELS

If the fluid drive does not turn freely, try to figure out what is binding it.

Remove the fluid drive from the motor by simply removing the two screws holding the fluid drive to the clutch lever. Pull the fluid drive straight off the shaft. Hold the clutch cone and turn the fluid drive housing around it. It should turn freely. If so, the bearings are probably good, and the motor shaft is probably bent. If the housing does NOT turn freely, the fluid drive is bad. Replace the defective component.

When re-installing the fluid drive, you must adjust the clutch lever as shown in figure S-6. First, loosen the cam

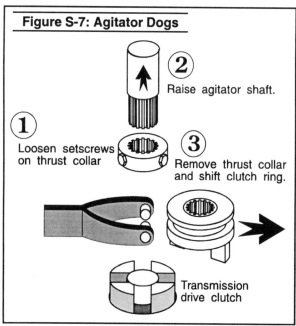

Figure S-7: Agitator Dogs

① Loosen setscrews on thrust collar

② Raise agitator shaft.

③ Remove thrust collar and shift clutch ring.

Transmission drive clutch

bolt locknut. Hold the solenoid plunger all the way down (retracted) and adjust the cam bolt until you have 1/8" of space between the lever end and the solenoid plunger extension (Figure S-6.) Then tighten the cam bolt locknut, but be careful not to tighten it too much. You don't want it to bind the movement of the lever.

8-7 SOLENOIDS (Early Models Only)

If the spin or agitate solenoid is not working, remove it from the machine and test it for continuity as described in section 2-5(a) and 1-4(b). Test also for any stickiness in its movement. Replace if defective.

If it appears to be good, check to see if you are getting voltage to it. This may entail running the machine while the cabinet is open, so be careful not to shock yourself, or injure yourself on any of the moving parts inside. Use your alligator jumpers to extend your test leads, and make sure that THEY are clear of any moving parts before you put power on the machine or start it.

If you have no voltage, stop the machine, break out the wiring diagram and start tracing wires and switches as described in section 2-5!

8-8 AGITATOR DOGS

To replace worn agitator dogs (aka shift clutch) you must pull up on the agitator shaft slightly.

First, remove the agitator as described in section 8-9.

Right above the agitator dogs, you'll see a thrust collar with two setscrews. (Figure S-7) Loosen the setscrews and lift up on the agitator shaft a few inches. The dogs and collar will fall off.

Installation is the opposite of removal, with one small adjustment. Beneath the drive block is a steel washer. (Figure S-8) Between that washer and the bearing surface at the top of the agitator post, there should be 12-thousandths (.012") clearance.

With the feeler gauge in place, push the thrust collar up against the bearing at the bottom of the centerpost, and tighten the setscrews.

8-9 AGITATOR SHAFT AND DRIVE BLOCK

To remove the agitator, simply unscrew the hold-down cap and lift it out.

Disconnect the agitator shaft as described in section 8-8 and draw the agitator shaft all the way out of the agitator post. When removing or installing the shaft, be very careful not to damage the seal near the top of the post (about 1/2" down the inside of the post.)

When the drive block wears out in these machines, you just replace the whole agitator shaft. Believe it or not, they're pretty cheap.

8-10 TUB REMOVAL/TUB SEALS, SEDIMENT TUBE

Remove the agitator and agitator driveshaft as described in section 8-9.

Remove the four bolts holding the agitator post and the basket to the spin tube. (Figure S-9) Carefully lift out the tub. (Take care not to damage the lid switch arm, or any other protrusion into the tub.

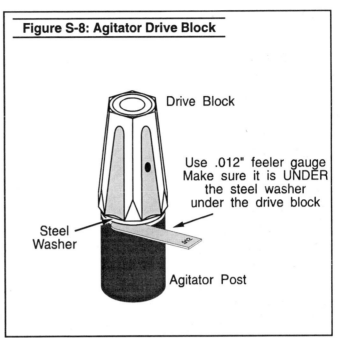

Figure S-8: Agitator Drive Block

Drive Block

Use .012" feeler gauge
Make sure it is UNDER the steel washer under the drive block

Steel Washer

Agitator Post

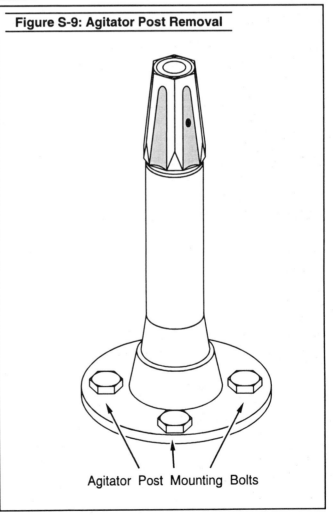

Figure S-9: Agitator Post Removal

Agitator Post Mounting Bolts

The boot seal forms the seal between the centerpost and the tub. It is held in place by two large clamps (Figure S-10) *Do not remove the clamps unless you intend to replace the seal.* Inspect the seal; if it is torn or appears brittle or caked with detergent, replace it.

Assembly is the opposite of disassembly. Always use new agitator post gaskets.

SEDIMENT TUBE

These machines had a solid wash basket with a row of holes around the upper rim. The wash basket contained all of the wash water, and none got into the tub until the spin cycle, when centrifugal force made it climb up the sides of the basket and flow out the holes.

Since there is no waterflow out the bottom of the basket, sand and sediment that settles there during the agitate cycle may not be able to work its way up the side of the basket (past the clothing) during the spin cycle, and thus may build up over time. The designers of these solid-basket machines were apparently concerned about this sand and sediment buildup in the bottom of the basket, and made provisions for preventing it.

A sediment tube (Figure S-11) goes outside the tub, from the bottom hub to the top of the tub. During the spin cycle, water plus any sediment that has accumulated will flow through the sediment tube into the tub, and out through the pump and drain.

This sediment tube can get brittle over the years and break. This will cause a water leak from the basket into the tub during the agitate cycle, and since the pump is turning all the time, it will be pumped out immediately. Thus it will seem like the tub keeps on draining throughout the agitate cycle.

If the tube comes loose from the clamp that holds it to the top of the tub, it will clatter around the tub during the spin cycle.

The solution is to remove the screws that hold it in place and replace the tube.

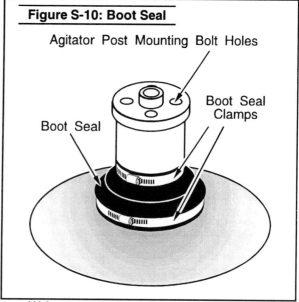

Figure S-10: Boot Seal

Agitator Post Mounting Bolt Holes

Boot Seal Clamps

Boot Seal

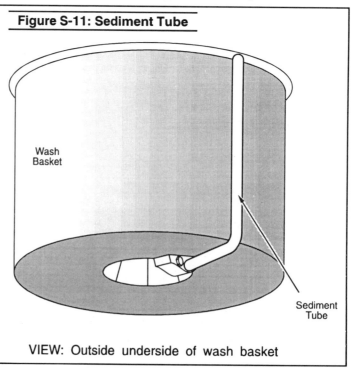

Figure S-11: Sediment Tube

Wash Basket

Sediment Tube

VIEW: Outside underside of wash basket

Chapter 8a

LATE MODEL (Post-1980) SPEED QUEEN / AMANA

Speed Queen has undergone several major design changes in the past few years. There are still significant numbers of all different designs out there, and they are generally not too expensive to repair, so all are included in this manual. In this book, they will be referred to as early model, middle model and late model machines. (also see Chapter 8)

Raytheon / Amana is notorious for making several design changes even within a single model year. When ordering or buying parts, it is wise to bring with you the production number, found on the nameplate along with the model number. Might save you a trip.

Your first duty is to figure out which machine you have. If you are not sure of when the machine was built, please read the first few paragraphs of Chapter 8 to determine what kind of machine you have.

Even among the new style machines, there have already been two MAJOR design changes. Inside the tub, they went from the old-style agitator post and drive block (similar to those found on old- and middle-model fluid drive machines) to a short-shaft air-bell agitator connection. (See section 8a-5) Later, they went from a pump driven by a second belt to one mounted directly on the drive motor.

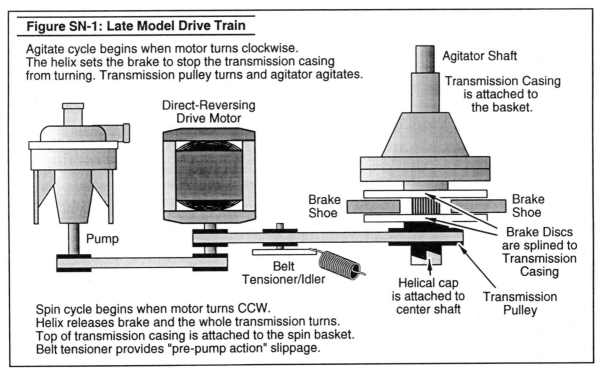

Figure SN-1: Late Model Drive Train

Agitate cycle begins when motor turns clockwise.
The helix sets the brake to stop the transmission casing from turning. Transmission pulley turns and agitator agitates.

Direct-Reversing Drive Motor

Pump

Belt Tensioner/Idler

Agitator Shaft

Transmission Casing is attached to the basket.

Brake Shoe

Brake Shoe

Brake Discs are splined to Transmission Casing

Helical cap is attached to center shaft

Transmission Pulley

Spin cycle begins when motor turns CCW.
Helix releases brake and the whole transmission turns.
Top of transmission casing is attached to the spin basket.
Belt tensioner provides "pre-pump action" slippage.

8a-1 BASIC OPERATING SYSTEMS

Late model machines have a direct-reversing motor, and the transmission is belt-driven directly off a motor pulley. (Figure SN-1) Until the early '90's they used a second belt to drive the pump; these are commonly referred to in the parts stores as "two-belt" machines. After that, the pump was driven directly off the bottom end of the motor shaft; these are commonly referred to as "direct drive" machines. There is only one belt in direct drive machines.

The top of the transmission casing is connected to the basket, and during the spin cycle, the whole transmission rotates. Slippage in the belt, allowed by the tensioner, permits a "pre-pump" action, allowing the basket to come slowly up to speed.

The bottom of the transmission casing is connected to a brake. This brake is activated by a helix in the hub of the transmission pulley. During the agitate cycle, the brake engages and prevents the transmission casing (and thus the basket) from turning. During the spin cycle, the helix mechanism releases the brake and the whole transmission spins around.

8a-2 OPENING THE CABINET AND CONSOLE

The console or cabinet may be opened as shown in figure SN-2.

CONSOLE SWITCHES

The timer knob simply unscrews from the timer shaft. Most other knobs pull straight off their D-shaped shafts. The timer and most other switches can then be removed by opening the console and removing the switches' terminals and appropriate mounting screws or nuts.

However, some switches on late model machines are different. To remove them from the console, you must press on the locking tabs adjacent to the shaft (figure SN-3) and twist the whole switch counterclockwise.

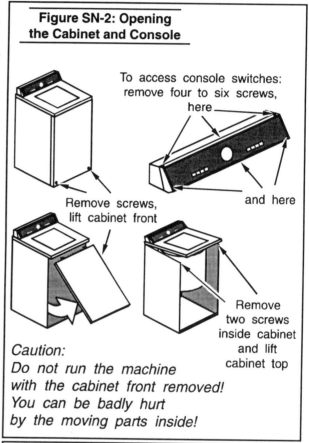

Figure SN-2: Opening the Cabinet and Console

To access console switches: remove four to six screws, here

and here

Remove screws, lift cabinet front

Remove two screws inside cabinet and lift cabinet top

Caution:
Do not run the machine with the cabinet front removed! You can be badly hurt by the moving parts inside!

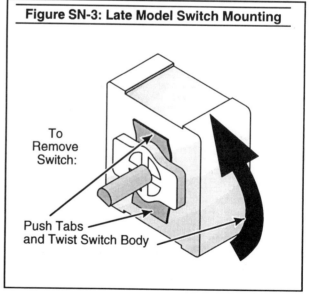

Figure SN-3: Late Model Switch Mounting

To Remove Switch:

Push Tabs and Twist Switch Body

8a-3 DIAGNOSIS

The most common problems with these washers are:

WATER LEAKS

In "short shaft" machines (late model machines with a drive bell; see section 8a-5) the center tub seal starts leaking. To repair or replace, see section 8a-6.

Another source of water on the floor is pump leaks. To replace, see section 8a-4.

The basket may be spinning during agitation. This will sling water over the top edge of the tub and appear to be a water leak.Replace the brake pads as described in section 8a-7.

NOISY OPERATION

In my opinion, these machines operate a little noisily to begin with. However, if they seem a little noisier than usual, check your belt(s). The sound is difficult to describe; it's kind of a "thunk-thunk-thunk." It happens when the belt has a few chunks taken out of it; the belt tensioner/idler starts "bouncing." To check and replace the belt, see section 8a-4.

A "knocking" sound during agitation may be a worn drive block. See section 8a-6.

OIL IN THE CLOTHES

If oil starts showing up in the clothes, what has usually happened is that the top transmission seal has deteriorated and is letting water into the transmission casing. The water displaces the oil and forces it out through the seal and into the clothes. If you want to keep the machine, the transmission must be replaced. This is a difficult and expensive repair, often costing more than 200 dollars just for parts. You may want to price out the job before you start and decide whether it might be more worthwhile to just replace the machine. You might also check out the availability of a rebuilt transmission. See section 8a-7.

NO AGITATE, OR NO SPIN

This is usually a broken transmission drive belt. (Section 8a-4) It could also be a defective drive motor. (Section 2-5(e)) or a siezed pump, preventing the motor from turning.

8a-4 PUMPS AND BELT CHANGING (Figure SN-4)

Pumps in the late model machines cannot be rebuilt. They must be replaced if leaking or defective.

TWO-BELT MACHINES

Belt driven pumps are replaced by simply removing the pump mounts.

Tension is kept on the pump belt by adjustment. Tension is kept on the transmission belt by an idler pulley. There is a kit available from your parts dealer with a new belt and idler and instructions on how to adjust the belt.

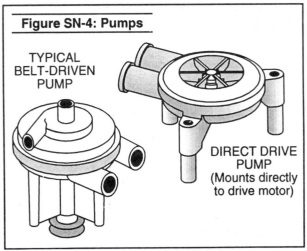

Figure SN-4: Pumps

TYPICAL BELT-DRIVEN PUMP

DIRECT DRIVE PUMP (Mounts directly to drive motor)

In two-belt machines, you can adjust the pump belt by loosening the pump mounting plate bolts and moving the pump until you have about 1/2-inch deflection with moderate finger pressure (about 1 to 2 pounds.)

DIRECT DRIVE MACHINES

Pump or belt changing on a direct drive machine is a little trickier. To do either the pump or belt, you must remove the motor platform. First, unplug the motor electrical harness block from the motor. Release belt tension by slipping the belt off the transmission pulley. Disconnect the hoses from the pump. (Water will run out, so have a towel handy!) You can then remove the four motor platform mounting screws, and rock the motor and pump assembly out. When you get it out, flip it upside down to work on the pump. (Figure SN-5)

Remove the screws mounting the pump to the motor. Sometimes the pump can get siezed up pretty good on the motor shaft and make the pump difficult to remove. Do not whack it; steady firm musclepower will get it off. Wiggle it just a little if you must.

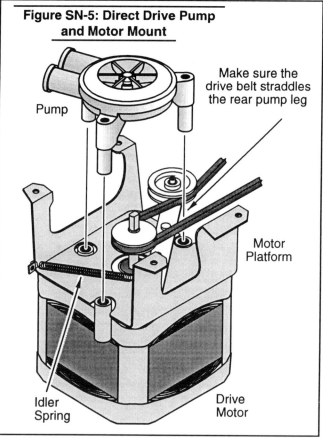

Figure SN-5: Direct Drive Pump and Motor Mount

Pump

Make sure the drive belt straddles the rear pump leg

Motor Platform

Idler Spring

Drive Motor

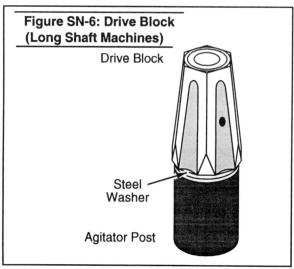

Figure SN-6: Drive Block (Long Shaft Machines)

Drive Block

Steel Washer

Agitator Post

When you put the new pump back on the motor, make sure the belt goes around the pulley and straddles the rear pump mounting leg. (Figure SN-5) Attach the motor platform to the baseplate using the four motor mounting screws. Make sure the belt is positioned inside the idler, and slip the belt around the transmission pulley. Then connect the hoses and motor wiring harness.

8a-5 AGITATOR ATTACHMENT: DRIVE BLOCK OR DRIVE BELL

Please note that two different methods were used to mount the agitator in these machines. Please read this entire section and determine which you have before trying to remove the agitator, or you may damage the machine, or even yourself!

EARLY TWO-BELT "LONG-SHAFT" MACHINES

The early two-belt machines had an agitator post and drive block much like the fluid drive machines. (figure SN-6) In these, you remove the agitator by unscrewing the hold down cap and lifting it out. You must remove the whole agitator post to get out the agitator shaft and drive block. (Figure SN-7) Remove the four bolts at the base of the agitator post and lift out the post. A circlip on the bottom of it holds the shaft in place. Remove it and the shaft will slide out of the post. Be careful not to damage the water seal inside the post when removing or installing the shaft.

When installing the post, be sure to use a new base gasket; it is one of the seals that keeps water away from the top of the transmission.

DRIVE BELL OR "SHORT SHAFT" MACHINES

In later machines, the agitator simply snaps onto a "drive bell." There is no screw cap holding the agitator on in these machines. To remove this agitator, the factory recommends a special tool. I have found it just as easy to take your belt off, slip it around the underside of the agitator and tug sharply upwards on the belt. (If you're *thick* enough, like me!) (Figure SN-8) Position the belt beneath the agitator vanes to avoid breaking the agitator. Be careful when you do this, or the agitator may hit you in the face when it pops off!

Once you've got the agitator off, you'll see the small plastic drive bell. (figure SN-8) This drive bell serves a couple of different functions. It connects the agitator to the agitator shaft of the transmission. It also traps air be-

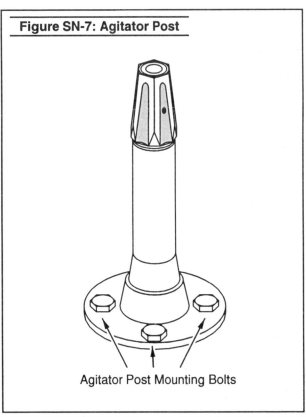

Figure SN-7: Agitator Post

Agitator Post Mounting Bolts

Figure SN-8: Agitator Removal and Drive Bell

Place belt beneath agitator and tug upwards sharply. there is a special tool sold for this, but the belt around your waist will do (If you're THICK enough!)

BE CAREFUL! It comes up fast and it can pop you in the face!

Basket

Drive Hub

Basket Mounting Bolts

Drive Bell (Hub Nut is underneath)

neath it and keeps water away from the seal and out of the transmission. There is an "O"-ring around the drive bell mounting screw, and/or a rubber plug that plugs the top of the drive bell, that seals the air inside the drive bell. It is critically important that this "O"-ring or plug be in good condition or water will get into the transmission and ruin it. Whenever you remove the drive bell screw, replace the "O"-ring or plug.

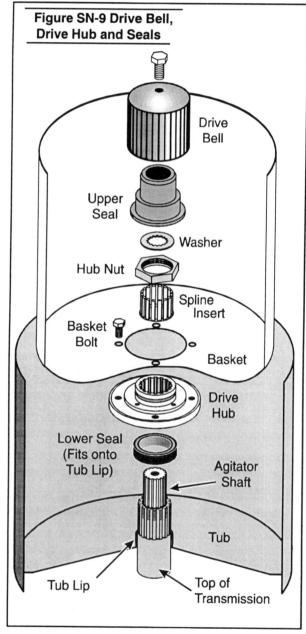

Figure SN-9 Drive Bell, Drive Hub and Seals

Drive Bell

Upper Seal

Washer

Hub Nut

Spline Insert

Basket Bolt

Basket

Drive Hub

Lower Seal (Fits onto Tub Lip)

Agitator Shaft

Tub

Tub Lip

Top of Transmission

Once you remove the mounting screw, the drive bell can be difficult to get off. If you can't get it off by hand, you have a couple of options. The factory sells a special puller; however, since a new drive bell comes with the seal kit, I've found that it's cheaper and easier to chisel off the old drive bell. With a cold chisel, just cut two slots along the hub of the drive bell to loosen it from the splined shaft beneath. Be careful not to chisel anywhere near the screw threads, or you might damage them.

Beneath the drive bell is a water seal. To remove it, pry up on the bottom of this seal with a screwdriver. The factory has a special tool to install it evenly, but if you're careful, you can do it by hand. Use some liquid dishsoap to lubricate it. The new seal kit comes with pretty thorough instructions.

8a-6 BASKET REMOVAL AND TUB WATER SEAL REPLACEMENT

If you are replacing the tub water seal, make sure you get the upper seal kit and replace it, too. It may be included with the lower seal kit; just make sure it's there.

First, remove the agitator and agitator post assembly, or the drive bell and seal, as described in section 8a-5.

Using a screwdriver, pop the tub ring clips holding the plastic tub ring to the top of the tub, slowly lifting up on the tub ring as you work your way around it. Remove the tub ring. Note the locator tabs in the ring and slots in the tub for reinstallation. Always replace the tub ring gasket; it should be included in your new seal kit.

If you just want to check the tub fittings, remove the four (or eight) basket bolts holding the basket to the drive hub and lift out the basket. Do not remove the hub nut.

If you are replacing the tub water seal, you will need to remove the drive hub. The hub is held onto the top of the transmission casing by either a hex nut or a spanner nut. Some have locking tabs you must bend out of the way first. You should then be able to turn the nut. There is a spanner available for this, but you can use a pipe wrench. Just be *extra* careful not to booger the threads with the pipe wrench; these threads are cut into the top of the transmission casing, and you *don't* want to have to buy a new *transmission.*

The water seal is beneath the drive hub. Note carefully the order and orientation in which things come off; there are some models out there with an parts that are slightly different than shown in Figure SN-9. Always replace used gaskets or seals.

There are a couple of surfaces to put sealant and lubricant on in replacing the water seal; the seal kit contains these. There is also a spline insert and a stainless steel sleeve to get in the right place. (The fingers of the spline insert point *upwards*!) The new hub and seal kit for your machine comes with instructions for installing the seal; follow them carefully.

8a-7 BRAKE AND TRANSMISSION SERVICE

If you just need to replace the brake pads, it is possible (but difficult!) to do so without removing the module from the machine. The problem is holding the transmission and getting a good grip on and turning the pulley at the same time; once the brake starts to release, the transmission will be free to turn. Then once you get the brake released, the problem becomes holding it in that position while you replace the brake pads. If you're going to try, make sure you remove the motor platform first to get more room to work.

If you need to replace the transmission or brake disk assembly, or the upper or lower bearings, you will need to remove the tub and transmission module.

To do this, first remove the wash basket, hub and tub water seal as described in previous sections.

Mark the front side of the tub with a piece of tape, so that you can reinstall it more easily. Remove the two front levelling springs by unhooking them from the tub. The factory sells a tool for releasing the springs, but you can fashion one out of a coathanger, or simply remove one of the front springs and use the hook on it to remove the other springs.

When you've got the springs off, disconnect the pressure hose from behind the tub. Rock the tub forward and out of the machine and flip the module upside down.

*(**Note**: DO NOT lubricate the pivot friction pads! Any lubrication on the friction pads will cause the machine to trip the out-of-balance switch too easily!)*

Disassembly of the module is pretty straightforward; see figure SN-10. However, there are one or two tips and tricks:

The brake spring must be seated in the notch in the transmission casing. The factory makes a special tool for this; however, it is possible (but difficult) to get the spring on with a couple of flat-bladed screwdrivers. It's your call. I say buy the tool if it's available.

Coat all transmission surfaces that contact the upper and lower bearings with an anti-sieze compound.

Make sure you mark the position of the balancing ring when you remove it from the transmission, so that you can get it back on the new transmission in the same way.

Figure SN-10 Module Assembly

NOTE:
Module assembly
is pictured upside-down;
this is the way
you will have it
when disassembling it!

ALSO NOTE:
There were many different models
made of this basic design! Some
had variations of the parts you see
here. For example, in some earlier
models, a needle bearing was used
in place of the thick and thin washers. In others, a cup-shaped drive
pulley was used. When disassembling, Note carefully the order and
orientation of the parts you remove
(draw pictures or take notes if you
must!) so you can get them back on
the same way.

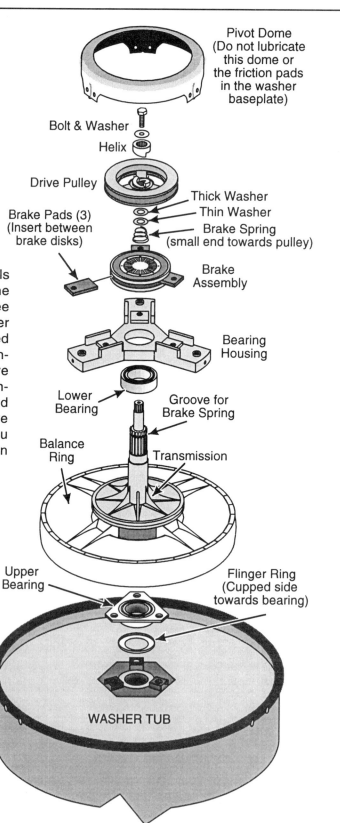

Pivot Dome
(Do not lubricate
this dome or
the friction pads
in the washer
baseplate)

Bolt & Washer

Helix

Drive Pulley

Thick Washer
Thin Washer
Brake Spring
(small end towards pulley)

Brake Pads (3)
(Insert between
brake disks)

Brake
Assembly

Bearing
Housing

Lower
Bearing

Groove for
Brake Spring

Balance
Ring

Transmission

Upper
Bearing

Flinger Ring
(Cupped side
towards bearing)

WASHER TUB

Chapter 9

NORGE DESIGNS

including Admiral, Magic Chef, Crosley, Maytag (Performa Models), and Signature (Montgomery Ward)

Please note that the Norge design has changed hands several times in the last couple of years. In the latest incarnation, Maycor is putting out their version of the Norge design as "Performa" model Maytag machines, as well as Magic Chef, Admiral and Crosley brands. Also note that Signature (Montgomery Ward) machines were, at various times over the last 20 years or so, built to either a Norge or Frigidaire/WCI design. Please look at both this chapter and chapter 10, WCI, and figure out what kind of machine you have *before* you try to diagnose it!

9-1 BASIC OPERATION (Figure N-1)

Norge machines use a direct reversing drive motor to change from agitate to spin cycles. Single, two- and three-speed motors were used in various models. Power is transmitted to the pump and transmission by a single belt. The motor is mounted on plastic mounts that slide in tracks in the baseplate of the machine. A large spring pushes the motor in its sliding tracks to keep tension on the belt. During the spin cycle, the whole transmission casing spins around; a clutch built into the transmission allows the transmission to

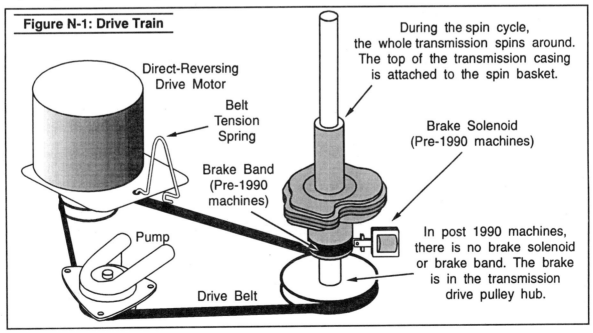

Figure N-1: Drive Train

Direct-Reversing Drive Motor

Belt Tension Spring

Brake Band (Pre-1990 machines)

Pump

Drive Belt

During the spin cycle, the whole transmission spins around. The top of the transmission casing is attached to the spin basket.

Brake Solenoid (Pre-1990 machines)

In post 1990 machines, there is no brake solenoid or brake band. The brake is in the transmission drive pulley hub.

accelerate slowly, allowing for a "pre-pump" action. During the agitate cycle, a brake keeps the transmission from spinning, and the gears inside the transmission operate the agitator.

Before 1990, these machines used a solenoid-operated brake band around the base of the transmission housing to stop the transmission from spinning. In more recent models, a cam in the transmission pulley hub allows the brake to engage when the motor is turning in the "agitate" direction, but releases it when the motor turns in the "spin" direction. For the purposes of this book, these machines will be referred to as pre-1990 or post-1990 machines, identifiable by the presence or absence of a brake band at the bottom of the transmission housing. (Figure N-1a)

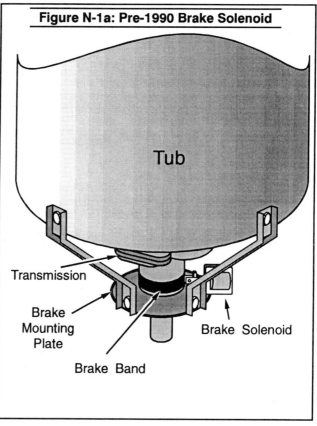

Figure N-1a: Pre-1990 Brake Solenoid

Tub

Transmission

Brake Mounting Plate

Brake Band

Brake Solenoid

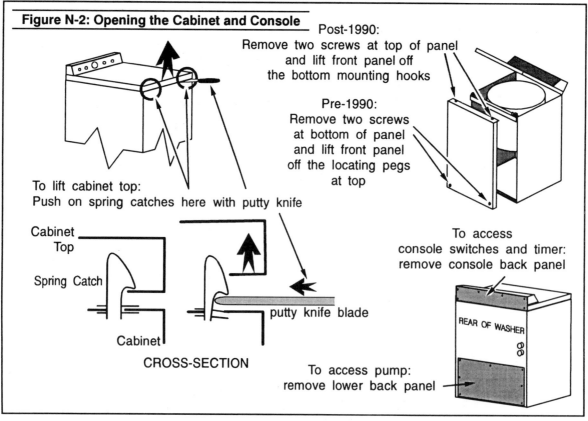

Figure N-2: Opening the Cabinet and Console

Post-1990:
Remove two screws at top of panel and lift front panel off the bottom mounting hooks

Pre-1990:
Remove two screws at bottom of panel and lift front panel off the locating pegs at top

To lift cabinet top:
Push on spring catches here with putty knife

Cabinet Top

Spring Catch

Cabinet

CROSS-SECTION

putty knife blade

To access console switches and timer:
remove console back panel

REAR OF WASHER

To access pump:
remove lower back panel

In pre-1990 models, the machine does not start spinning until the tub is partially pumped out. This is accomplished in one of two ways. In most machines, the timer holds the brake for a minute and a half or so at the beginning of the spin cycle while the pump starts draining the tub. In just a few models, a "dashpot" was used. It looks like a diaphragm switch mounted piggyback to the brake solenoid. It is simply a pressure switch that senses water level in the tub, and releases the brake at the appropriate water level. Replace if defective. In a few very old pre-1990 machines, there is a solenoid-activated clutch that works in conjunction with the brake. (I don't know if there are still any operating out there; frankly, I've never seen any.)

9-2 OPENING THE CABINET AND CONSOLE

The cabinet and console may be opened for service as shown in figure N-2. Please note that the front panel cannot be lifted off the machine until the cabinet top has been raised.

9-3 DIAGNOSIS

Well, we have good news and bad news here. The good news is that Norge design machines are pretty tough and seem to last at least a good 8 to 10 years. The bad news is that transmission, tub seal or upper (spin) bearing repairs are extremely difficult and expensive and require many special tools, and thus *usually* render the machine not economically worth repairing.

Here are the most common problems with these machines:

PUMP AND/OR BELT PROBLEMS

Leaking pumps are the single most common problem with this machine, and they are easy to replace. See section 9-4.

If the machine is not pumping, there may not be enough belt tension on the pump belt; check for a broken belt or tensioning spring. The belt is subject to normal wear as described in Chapter 2, section 2-4(a). If you have belt wear problems, also check the motor tracks and belt-tensioning spring as described in section 9-5. The motor tracks may be mucked up or corroded, preventing the motor from "floating" in its track enough to tension the belt.

NO SPIN OR SLOW SPIN, OR NO AGITATION

This may be caused by a number of different problems. The first thing to determine is whether or not the motor is turning. If not, you may have timer or motor problems, or speed selector switch or lid switch problems as described in Chapter 2. If the motor *is* turning, you may have brake bearing or spin bearing problems; see sections 9-6 and 9-7.

NOISES

A squeak during braking in post-1990 models can be solved by sanding the rotor drum surface lightly with emery cloth, but it is not an easy job. The brake spring is heavily pre-loaded and requires some special tools to remove and install safely. See section 9-6.

A rattling noise can indicate a worn flexible rubber bushing in the motor drive pulley hub. See section 9-6.

A rumbling sound is usually an upper (spin) bearing problem. This may also come across as a sound like a jet engine or a Ferrari taking off as the machine accelerates into the spin cycle (an accelerating whe-e-e-e sound). This is often accompanied by water leaking from the tub seal above the transmission; look around the inside walls of the cabinet for signs of water slinging off the transmission during the spin cycle. See section 9-7. In pre-1990 models, a rumbling or growling sound can also indicate bad bearings in the transmission drive pulley assembly. See section 9-6.

VIBRATION

Vibration in these machines usually occurs because of bleach leaks. There is a bleach dispensing cup molded into the top of the tub ring. Bleach spits out of this cup, and drips down around the baseplate of the washer. The baseplate and cabinet quickly rust, and the baseplate suspension spring mounts or even the suspension springs themselves may crack or break. If a suspension spring on one side is broken or disabled, the washer will vibrate badly.

You can try to replace a broken suspension spring (if you must replace one, you must replace the whole set). However, it can be very difficult, and it requires expensive special tools. Normally there is no repair for this problem. If the baseplate of the washer is badly corroded, you will probably end up scrapping the washer soon.

BRAKE AND BRAKE SOLENOID

In pre-1990 models, if the basket tries to spin with the tub full of water, the brake is not engaging. You will find the brake assembly mounted to the plate near the bottom of the transmission (Figure N-1a). Check the brake solenoid and dashpot (if installed) Also check the linkage and the brake band. Test the solenoid as described in section 2-5(a). Replace if defective.

Though the brake solenoid is relatively easy to replace, the brake band is extremely difficult, requiring special tools. If the lining or band needs service, or if the brake is squealing, call a qualified service technician or junk the washer.

9-4 PUMP (Figure N-3)

The pump is accessed through the rear cabinet panel. To remove it, simply remove two hoses, then the three screws that hold it in place. When installing, reach underneath and make sure the belt is properly seated on the pump, motor and transmission pullies.

9-5 MOTOR MOUNTS AND BELT TENSION

The motor is mounted in two plastic mounts (Figure N-4) which slide into slots in the motor base. Make sure these tracks are free of any detergent buildup or anything else that might restrict the free movement of the motor. Also check that the belt tensioning spring is in the right place (Figure N-4) and is not broken.

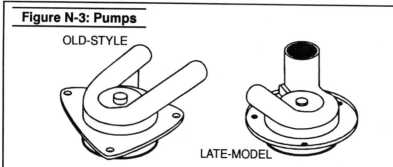

Figure N-3: Pumps
OLD-STYLE
LATE-MODEL

9-6 MOTOR PULLEY AND TRANSMISSION PULLEY

Some of these machines used a motor pulley with a flexible rubber hub which tends to disintegrate after a few years. If the pulley literally flops around on its hub with the belt tension removed from it, that's what's happened. Replacements are available; to remove the pulley, remove the setscrew as shown in figure N-4.

Some late model machines have a nylon/fiberglass motor pulley that is pressed onto a splined motor shaft. It can be replaced if damaged, but it requires a puller to get it off. Reinstalling it, tap it onto the motor shaft with a 1/2 inch socket until it bottoms on the shoulder on the motor shaft. To prevent motor bearing damage when you tap it on, make sure you remove the plastic shaft cover on the other end of the motor and back up the shaft against something solid. (Like a wall or workbench.)

In pre-1990 models, the transmission drive pulley and its bearing are located in the center of the baseplate. The bearing within the plate can get rusted or worn, causing noise and excessive belt wear. They are difficult to replace. If this happens, call a qualified service technician.

The transmission drive pulley in post-1990 machines is made of a plastic material. The bearing assembly is pictured in figure N-5. When disassembling this assembly, count the pieces beneath the pulley; there should be six. When this bearing gets severely worn, the lower washer will embed itself into the plastic pulley, and you may only count five pieces. There may be powdered plastic or metal residue or pieces of the pulley on the other bearing assembly parts. The symptom will be that

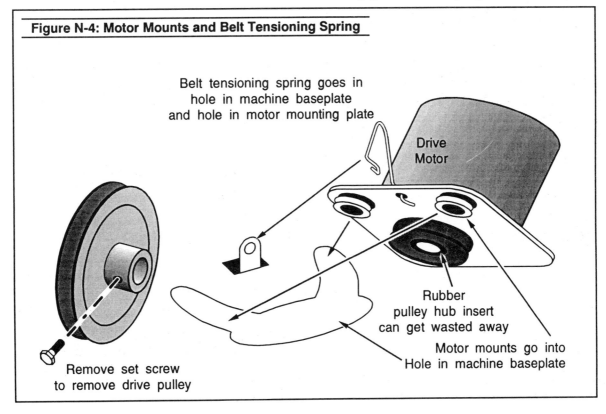

Figure N-4: Motor Mounts and Belt Tensioning Spring

Belt tensioning spring goes in hole in machine baseplate and hole in motor mounting plate

Drive Motor

Remove set screw to remove drive pulley

Rubber pulley hub insert can get wasted away

Motor mounts go into Hole in machine baseplate

the basket is not spinning; the reason is that due to the wear in this bearing, the brake is not lifting enough to release and allow the transmission to spin. A kit is available to replace the pulley and bearing assembly.

You *may* need to adjust the brake release. After you replace the bearing assembly, turn the pulley CCW until the brake releases. Look at the reference marks on the lower cam; the brake should release when the drive pulley hub shoulder is between 3 and 9 marks on the lower cam. Less than 3, and you need to replace the .062 thrust washer with a .032 thrust washer. If the brake releases at more than 9 marks, install both the .032 thrust washer and the .062 washer.

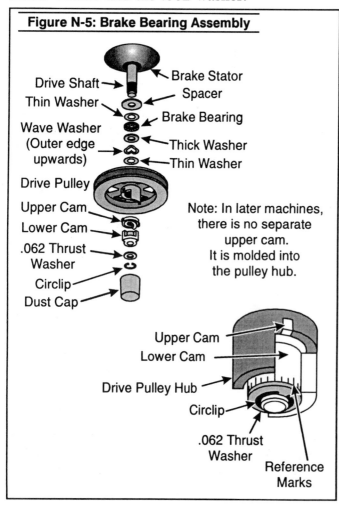

Figure N-5: Brake Bearing Assembly

Drive Shaft
Thin Washer
Wave Washer (Outer edge upwards)
Drive Pulley
Upper Cam
Lower Cam
.062 Thrust Washer
Circlip
Dust Cap

Brake Stator
Spacer
Brake Bearing
Thick Washer
Thin Washer

Note: In later machines, there is no separate upper cam. It is molded into the pulley hub.

Upper Cam
Lower Cam
Drive Pulley Hub
Circlip
.062 Thrust Washer
Reference Marks

Brake squeaking can usually be quieted by removing the brake housing and lightly sanding the metal rotor drum surface with emery cloth to break the glaze. However, the brake spring is loaded to 200 pounds and requires a special tool (number 35-2442) to remove. Your parts distributor *may* have one in stock, but for most distributors it is usually a special order.

9-7 TRANSMISSION

If you have upper or lower spin bearing or tub seal leakage problems, you will probably end up junking the washer. The transmission is a real son-of-a-gun to remove. First, it takes about $200 worth of special tools, in addition to the parts cost. And speaking of parts costs, the upper bearing surface is the transmission casing itself, and usually the whole transmission must be replaced due to rust and wear. The suspension springs are heavily loaded and difficult and dangerous to remove. The set screw in the drive block is usually corroded so badly that it cannot be removed.

If you have symptoms that indicate a transmission problem, you might try calling a qualified service technician. However, be forewarned: *if* you can find a technician who's willing to do the job, it will probably cost you 350 dollars or more. Unless you're emotionally attached to the washer, it's usually not worth it. Sorry to be the bearer of bad tidings, but in my experience, you will usually end up getting rid of the machine.

Chapter 10

WCI
(White Consolidated Industries)

including Frigidaire, Franklin, Gibson, Kelvinator, late-model Montgomery Ward, Westinghouse and other brands

As you can guess by the subtitle of this chapter, WCI (White Consolidated Industries) seems to have undergone more than its share of mergers and acquisitions. Designs have been changed and dropped so fast that sometimes it's hard to stay on top of them all.

Frigidaire had some machines that were fairly popular and lasted a long time, so we still see a few around. These are the Uni-Matic, Pulse-Matic and Roller Drive Models. Unfortunately, they are difficult and expensive to get parts for, and there are so few left that they're not covered in this book.

In the past few years, WCI seems to have stuck with two different designs. These are referred to in this book (and in the parts houses) as the Westinghouse design and the Franklin design. Lately,

WCI seems to have combined the motor and pump from a Westinghouse design with the transmission from the Franklin machine.

Unless otherwise noted, a particular diagnosis or procedure explained in this book applies to either machine.

10-1 BASIC OPERATION

WESTINGHOUSE DESIGN

Westinghouse-designed machines (Figure WC-1) have a direct reversing motor. The pump is mounted directly to the top of the motor, and a pulley on the bottom of the motor drives the transmission through a belt. A spring-loaded belt tensioner/idler assembly keeps proper tension on the belt and provides for pre-pump action. A clutch mechanism is integral inside of the transmission.

FRANKLIN DESIGN

Franklin designs (Figure WC-2) also have a direct-reversing motor. The pump is mounted on the bottom of the motor shaft, beneath the motor pulley. The transmission is belt driven, with a tensioner/idler providing pre-pump ac-tion and keeping the proper belt tension. A clutch mechanism is integral inside of the transmission.

During the spin cycle, the whole transmission assembly spins. The basket is attached to the top of the transmission casing.

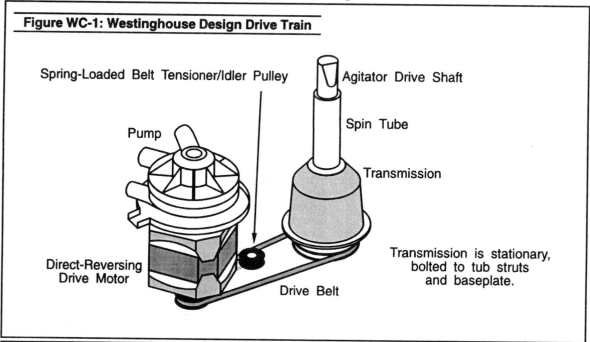

Figure WC-1: Westinghouse Design Drive Train

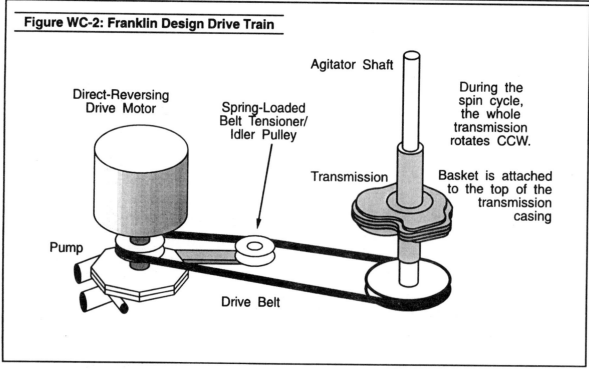

Figure WC-2: Franklin Design Drive Train

10-2 OPENING THE CABINET AND CONSOLE

The cabinet and console areas may be accessed as shown in figure WC-3. Note that the Franklin design is slightly different from the Westinghouse design; it has a lower front panel that can be removed to access the transmission and other components.

Figure WC-3: Opening the Cabinet and Console

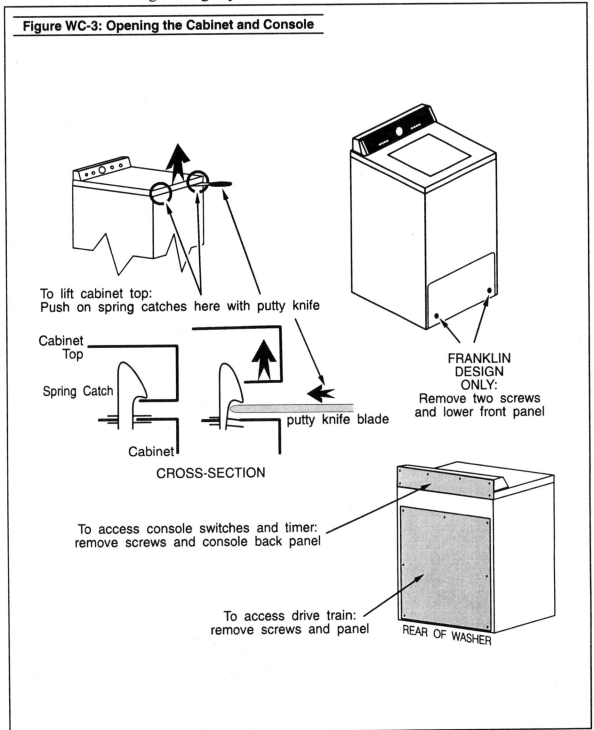

To lift cabinet top:
Push on spring catches here with putty knife

Cabinet Top
Spring Catch
Cabinet
putty knife blade
CROSS-SECTION

FRANKLIN DESIGN ONLY:
Remove two screws and lower front panel

To access console switches and timer:
remove screws and console back panel

To access drive train:
remove screws and panel

REAR OF WASHER

10-3 DIAGNOSIS

The most common problems with these machines are:

OIL LEAKS (Westinghouse Design Only)

These machines tend to develop an oil leak after a few years. The oil is very thick, and the leak is slow, but it really gets slung around so everything under the tub gets oily. The belt gets oily, too, and starts slipping and burning.

The bottom oil seal is quite difficult for a novice to replace, so your options are limited:

1) Call a qualified service technician to replace the seal. If you're lucky, it will last another few years.

2) Junk the washer.

3) Do nothing. Clean up the oil, replace the belt, and keep running the machine. You will have to repeat the process in a few months, but it seems like these machines will just keep on chugging with almost no oil in them. When the transmission finally runs out of oil and dies (it may be years,) junk the washer.

DRIVE BLOCK

A knocking sound during the agitation cycle usually indicates a worn drive block. It can be replaced, but you need a wheel puller to get the old one off.

BELTS

The drive belts in these machines are subject to normal wear as described in section 2-4(a). Belt problems in Westinghouse designed machines can also be due to oil leaks (see OIL LEAKS above.) See section 10-4.

PUMPS

These machines experience the usual pump problems as described in section 2-3. Pumps on both designs are easily rebuildable. See section 10-5.

10-4 DRIVE BELT

Since drive belt tension is kept by a spring-loaded idler, replacement is easy.

First, note the notches that the tension springs are in. Proper belt adjustment is important in these machines, so make sure you get everything back in the same place.

Then simply slip the old belt off and the new one on.

If the belt is not adjusted properly, you may hear a clattering noise during spin (this is the idler touching the motor mounting plate; too loose) or you will notice excessive belt wear (too tight.)

10-5 PUMPS

Westinghouse-designed pumps are dramatically different from the Franklin designed pumps. Franklin pumps can be removed from the motor in one piece. Westinghouse pumps are an assembly with the motor, and in order to service them, the whole pump and motor assembly must be removed.

Both pumps have carbon seals which are sensitive to the distance of the pump body from the motor for proper sealing. The Westinghouse pump is particularly sensitive to this. When disassembling these pumps, note the exact position of every shim, grommet and washer. And be absolutely certain that every single one goes back in the same place, or your pump will leak. Also, make sure the carbon sealing rings stay absolutely clean; in fact, try not to even touch the sealing surfaces with clean fingers if you can avoid it. The Body oils and acids on your fingertips may etch the seal and shorten its life.

In disassembling these pumps, also note that some of the screws hold the pump body together, and some hold the pump body to the motor. Be careful when tightening the screws that hold the plastic pieces together; it's easy to strip plastic threads by overtightening. Snug is all you need. Let the gasket do its job.

After you re-assemble either pump, turn the motor over by hand and feel for any rubbing. If the impeller is rubbing the pump housing, the distance between the pump body and the motor must be shimmed according to the instructions that come with the pump rebuilding kit.

FRANKLIN PUMP (Figure WC-4)

These pumps can be removed from the motor by taking out the allen-head setscrew that holds the impeller to the motor shaft (Figure WC-4.) Then re-move the hoses and drop the pump off the motor shaft.

WESTINGHOUSE PUMP
(Figure WC-5)

When removing the motor and pump assembly, be extra careful not to get any water in the motor.

When re-assembling the pump, keep in mind that there are two sets of holes for mounting the pump body to the mo-tor. These holes are marked "G" and "W." The motors used in these machines came from two different suppliers, GE and Westinghouse, each of which had different pump body mounting holes. Either motor will replace the other, but to get the proper pump hose alignment, use the right set of holes.

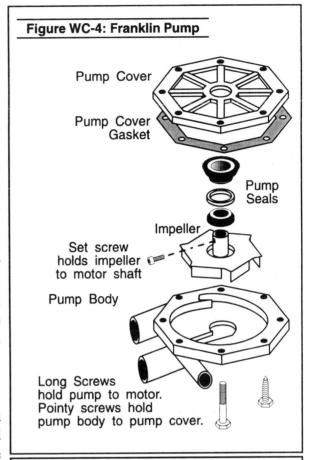

Figure WC-4: Franklin Pump

Pump Cover

Pump Cover Gasket

Pump Seals

Impeller

Set screw holds impeller to motor shaft

Pump Body

Long Screws hold pump to motor. Pointy screws hold pump body to pump cover.

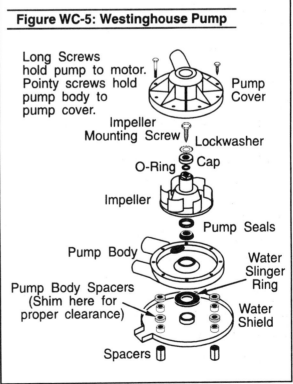

Figure WC-5: Westinghouse Pump

Long Screws hold pump to motor. Pointy screws hold pump body to pump cover.

Pump Cover

Impeller Mounting Screw

Lockwasher

O-Ring   Cap

Impeller

Pump Seals

Pump Body

Water Slinger Ring

Pump Body Spacers (Shim here for proper clearance)

Water Shield

Spacers

Index

Available from EB Publishing

Also Available from EB Publishing
Brand-Specific Dryer & Top-Loading Washer Manuals!
for those who want a little LESS...
Our brand-specific manuals have the same high quality instructions and illustrations
as our all-brand manuals, at a new low price!

2000 Edition

Whirlpool Dryer Repair
ISBN 1-890386-42-1   Part No. EBWD

2000 Edition

Whirlpool Washer Repair
ISBN 1-890386-41-3   Part No. EBWW

*Whirlpool-brand manuals include
Kenmore, Kitchenaid, Estate
and Roper Brand Machines*

2000 Edition

GE/Hotpoint Dryer Repair
ISBN 1-890386-44-8   Part No. EBGD

2000 Edition

GE/Hotpoint Washer Repair
ISBN 1-890386-43-X   Part No. EBGW

*GE-brand manuals include
Hotpoint, late-model RCA, and
JC Penney (Penncrest) Brand Machines*

2000 Edition

Maytag Dryer Repair
ISBN 1-890386-46-4   Part No. EBMD

2000 Edition

Maytag Washer Repair
ISBN 1-890386-45-6   Part No. EBMW